DATE DUE

Keys to
CURRICULUM
MAPPING

Keys to
CURRICULUM
MAPPING
Strategies and Tools to Make It Work

Susan Udelhofen

Foreword by
Heidi Hayes Jacobs

CORWIN PRESS
A SAGE Publications Company
Thousand Oaks, California

For information:

Corwin Press
A Sage Publications Company
2455 Teller Road
Thousand Oaks, California 91320
www.corwinpress.com

Sage Publications Ltd.
1 Oliver's Yard
55 City Road
London EC1Y 1SP
United Kingdom

Sage Publications India Pvt. Ltd.
B-42 Panchsheel Enclave
Post Box 4109
New Delhi 110 017 India

Printed in the United States of America

Library of Congress Cataloging-in-Publication Data

Udelhofen, Susan.
Keys to curriculum mapping: Strategies and tools to make it work / Susan Udelhofen; foreword by Heidi Hayes Jacobs.
    p. cm.
Includes bibliographical references and index.
ISBN 1-4129-0957-0 (cloth) — ISBN 1-4129-0958-9 (pbk.)
    1. Curriculum planning. 2. Curriculum evaluation. I. Title.
LB2806.15.U34 2005
375'.001—dc22   2004028778

This book is printed on acid-free paper.

05   06   07   08   09   10   9   8   7   6   5   4   3   2   1

Acquisitions Editor:	Jean Ward
Production Editor:	Diane S. Foster
Copy Editor:	Barbara Coster
Typesetter:	C&M Digitals (P) Ltd.
Proofreader:	Libby Larson
Indexer:	Teri Greenberg
Cover Designer:	Anthony Paular

Contents

List of Figures

Foreword

Recently I was on the phone with a school principal and was struck with the respect and enthusiasm emanating from his voice when he spoke about Susan Udelhofen. We were discussing his work on curriculum mapping. "Susan has worked with us. She has made such a difference with our faculty. They trust her. She is credible because she has this no-nonsense way of going to the heart of how to really make mapping work." It occurred to me that this is always the case with Susan. She is an exceptional educator and human being who inspires loyalty. There is wisdom in paying attention to her thinking, for she is consistently committed to the highest level of professionalism.

Vividly I remember my first encounter with Dr. Udelhofen in Orlando, Florida, about 10 years ago. I had just presented at a conference there and was putting my materials on my model for curriculum mapping back into my briefcase. An open and warm educator approached me with wonderful questions, new angles, and ideas for mapping. Clearly, this earnest and intelligent woman was someone to listen to. This person was Susan Udelhofen. I consider it an honor to be her colleague. She has extended and deepened the field of curriculum mapping.

The book you hold in your hands is filled with experience and insight into the curriculum mapping process. Based on her work as a teacher and consultant throughout the United States, she shares suggestions for the daunting task of getting started: how to engage your faculty, how to avoid the pitfalls, how to begin with an eye to the long view. Curriculum mapping is not the latest trend. It is a genuine shift in how we make decisions and communicate as professionals. By employing technology and rethinking what educators document and how they review and revise their curriculum, a 21st-century solution emerges.

Dr. Udelhofen has enriched this exciting new field in education. Mapping did not exist 10 years ago in the way that we think of it now, because we did not have the means of communicating as we do now. By bringing technology into every classroom and between classrooms K–12, we can replace our more dated ways of planning. But making the transition is tough, even daunting. Dr. Udelhofen's contribution in these pages will help any educator interested in bringing their faculty into the new time with new tools to help their learners.

Detailed coaching on the strategies for helping teachers enter data on maps with a strong understanding of each component on the maps is a highlight. One of the strongest features of the book is laying out ways to assist colleagues in communicating with one another about maps and assessment data. Dr. Udelhofen is always practical. She grapples with the intriguing and complex realities of a range of school settings: elementary, middle, and high school; the district office; private and public. She knows that "one size fits all" has never worked in education. This book will be of enormous help to staff developers, building and district administrators, and to classroom teachers at all levels of instruction.

One of Dr. Udelhofen's great strengths is mentoring, as evidenced in her first book, *The Mentoring Year* (2000). She has a knack for guiding us through the obstacles and challenges of mapping with a steadiness and practicality that is reassuring. In a sense we are mentored by this master educator as we read through the pages of *Keys to Curriculum Mapping: Strategies and Tools to Make it Work*.

—*Heidi Hayes Jacobs*

Acknowledgments

My deepest gratitude and respect to Heidi Hayes Jacobs for providing the Foreword. Her knowledge, encouragement, and generous spirit paved the way for this book and I am forever grateful.

My sincere appreciation goes to the following colleagues, friends, and family members for their support and expertise:

- Kathryn Udelhofen, my lovely daughter, who brought me Starbucks coffee and urged me to take breaks from my writing when she knew I needed them most.
- Jean Ward, Corwin Press Editor, for her encouragement, sound advice, meaningful feedback, and ongoing support.
- Dr. Jane Meyers, educator and very good friend, who gave up a portion of her Wisconsin vacation to read drafts and offer suggestions as I organized and completed my writing. I wish Arizona and Wisconsin were in closer proximity!
- Tim Peterson, curriculum expert and colleague who read the manuscript, offered thoughtful feedback, and provided a much needed sounding board.
- Greg and Claudia Quam, sister and brother-in-law and friends, who have dedicated their professional lives to education and offered valuable insight into this project.
- Ann Johnson, Associate Superintendent of Instruction and curriculum mapping expert, for generously sharing curriculum map samples.

The following educators and their respective faculties are at the heart of this book. They worked collaboratively with me as they implemented curriculum mapping in their districts, provided important curriculum mapping data, read drafts of the manuscript, and offered their feedback. This book would not have been possible without their help and I am very grateful.

- Sue Dohr, and Carol Topinka, Media Specialist and Curriculum Director, St. Francis School District, St. Francis, Wisconsin
- Patti Kunz, and Brenda Bredeson, media/curriculum director and teacher, Juda School District, Juda, Wisconsin
- Sue Pedro, Director of Elementary Curriculum and Instruction, Washington Local School District, Toledo, Ohio
- Tammy Bauck, Curriculum Director, South Dakota Department of Education, Pierre, South Dakota

- Kathy Hood, Curriculum Director, Spearfish School District, Spearfish, South Dakota
- Glenn Bugni, Director of Instruction and Achievement, Antigo School District, Antigo, Wisconsin
- David Bowman, Curriculum Director, Shawnee Heights School District, Tecumseh, Kansas
- The many teachers who shall remain unnamed but are much appreciated for sharing their stories

About the Author

 **Susan Udelhofen** is a national staff development leader providing consulting services to school districts, education agencies, universities, and colleges. Her work concentrates primarily on issues and practices related to curriculum mapping, teacher mentoring, assessment, standards, and program evaluation.

Dr. Udelhofen earned a doctorate in curriculum and instruction and an M.S. in educational psychology, both from the University of Wisconsin-Madison.

Her experience includes work at the Wisconsin Department of Public Instruction as a Goals 2000 consultant and gifted and talented consultant. She has taught courses in teacher mentoring, assessment, reading methods, children's literature, gifted and talented education, and also served as supervisor/instructor of preservice teachers at the University of Wisconsin-Madison. She is an experienced classroom teacher and holds current licensure.

She is the coauthor of *The Mentoring Year: A Step-by-Step Guide to Professional Development* (2003, Corwin Press) and *The Teacher Journal: Reflections About Teaching and Learning* (self-published).

Her presentation experience includes appearances at the National Staff Development Conference, Curriculum Mapping Institutes, New Teacher Center Symposium, American Research Association, National Reading Association, National School Conference Institute, and Wisconsin Association for Supervision and Curriculum Development.

She resides in Madison, Wisconsin, with her husband and is the mother of two college-aged children. She can be contacted by e-mail at su-consulting @charter.net or her Web site at su-consulting.com.

This book is dedicated to John, my husband and best friend,
for his support, encouragement, patience, and love. I am very lucky.

Introduction:
The Curriculum
Mapping Journey

G ood curriculum begins by asking all teachers to document the content and skills they teach and then providing opportunities for them to talk with one another about their *real* classroom teaching and how those practices affect our students. That was the message Heidi Hayes Jacobs shared with her audience at a national staff development conference in Orlando, Florida, in 1997. I was attending this session as a consultant for the Wisconsin State Department of Education and hoping to learn more about effective staff development. Little did I realize the profound ways that her thought-provoking perception of curriculum development would guide my professional journey.

As I listened to her that morning, I began to reflect upon my experiences as a classroom teacher and realized that I had never been asked what I really taught in the classroom. Certainly my colleagues and I shared anecdotal comments about lessons and activities, but we did not discuss specific content, skills, and assessment issues. As I thought about the concept of curriculum mapping, I realized what a powerful exercise it would have been for me, and my colleagues, to have had the opportunity to write about and discuss our real classroom practices. I feel certain that the teachers in my building would have worked more closely together, our discussions would have been richer, and, most important, student learning would have improved.

From that point I was determined to learn all I could about curriculum mapping. I attended curriculum mapping trainings, workshops, and conferences and read as much as I could about the process. I talked with numerous colleagues and educators who were leading teachers through the curriculum mapping steps. It was also at this time that I left the state department and started my own consulting practice, with a portion of it devoted to curriculum mapping.

Now, recalling those first districts I worked with to implement curriculum mapping, I realize how much I learned and better understand the many complexities associated with changing the historic structure of curriculum development. The culture of the school, previous curriculum work, teacher attitudes, administrative commitment, time, and technology support were issues that had profound influences on the successful implementation of curriculum mapping. What began as a relatively simple process I soon discovered was a very complex endeavor.

The purpose of this book is to help those who are beginning curriculum mapping and others who may be in the midst of implementation. The book presents the challenges and successes of curriculum mapping, strategies for implementation, and guidelines for long-term planning.

WHAT IS CURRICULUM MAPPING AND WHY IS IT IMPORTANT?

Curriculum mapping is a process by which all teachers document their own curriculum, then share and examine each other's curriculums for gaps, overlaps, redundancies, and new learning, creating a coherent, consistent, curriculum within and across schools that is ultimately aligned to standards and responsive to student data and other school initiatives. The concept of curriculum mapping originated in the 1980s with the work of Fenwick English, who defined curriculum mapping as a reality-based record of the content that is actually taught, how long it is being taught, and the match between what is taught and the district's assessment program (English, 1980). In the 1990s, Heidi Hayes Jacobs broadened English's definition of curriculum mapping and created a multiphased process for mapping the curriculum in her book *Mapping the Big Picture* (1997) and in her latest publication, *Getting Results With Curriculum Mapping* (2004). It is her concept of curriculum mapping that provides the basis for this practical guide, which connects curriculum mapping to current reform initiatives, and provides working templates that I have developed to help school teams with the process of digging into curriculum mapping and discussion, and true case stories of schools that have used this process to transform and revitalize teaching and learning.

Curriculum mapping is the process where each teacher records the content and skills taught and how they are assessed and aligned to academic standards. These data are recorded by the month, which provides a common reference point and time-bound element to the maps. Essential questions are also components on the maps that provide the overarching questions that hold the curriculum together and guide our instruction to help students better understand the content and make real-world connections. Following the data collection, teachers read one another's maps, come together in small and large groups to discuss what they discovered as they read the maps, and finally make recommendations and suggestions for curriculum reform. By collecting their own curriculum data and discussing it with peers, teachers see the vertical grade-to-grade curriculum relationships as well as the horizontal curriculum picture within a grade level. This reflective, shared process invites teachers to think, write, reflect, discuss, and revise curriculum in thoughtful and collaborative ways. It is a long-term, ongoing process, and while challenging, it is a journey with remarkable outcomes.

As Steffy and English (1997) suggest, curriculum is developed from any material a teacher refers to or uses to decide what to teach, when to teach it, and how much of it to teach. These sources or materials include the following:

- Textbooks
- Teachers' guides to textbooks
- School board directives
- Scope and sequence charts
- Curriculum guides
- State department guidelines
- National guidelines
- Administrator directives
- Supervisor recommendations
- Work plans
- Purchased education materials
- Prepackaged units and standards
- Personal interest/travel experiences

Often, these curriculum sources and practices are not documented in a consistent, comprehensive manner, nor are they shared among colleagues in meaningful ways. The result is an inconsistent, fragmented curriculum that does not optimize grade-to-grade, cross-content area learning experiences for our students.

Heidi Hayes Jacobs (1997) expanded curriculum mapping in four significant ways: (1) a time element was introduced where each teacher documented the curriculum elements by month, (2) coordination and review of the curriculum information was established among buildings, (3) assessment information was included, and (4) the curriculum information was entered electronically. This work provided a framework to map the curriculum and change traditional curriculum development.

As I learned more about the curriculum mapping process, I recalled my experiences as a second grade teacher and remembered a very large and significant gap in my curriculum: I didn't teach science. My science curriculum consisted of the science kits that sat unused in the back corner of my classroom. However, I felt I made up for my lack of science teaching with my stellar social studies units. I was convinced my students would get more than enough science education as they progressed to the upper grades. Although my elementary classroom experience occurred a number of years ago, this remains a relatively common occurrence in many of our schools today. While all teachers have areas of expertise and teaching preferences, we have to consider what is in the best interests of students. History suggests that for many teachers, a perception of "self-employment" is very common due to the isolated nature of the profession. This isolated approach to curriculum development and teaching practice pays little credence to the students' experiences beyond the scope of the individual teacher's classroom or to the current age of state-mandated standards and high accountability. Mapping the curriculum brings teachers out of isolation and provides a focused, reflective, and collaborative process that has a positive impact on all stakeholders—most important, on students, but also on teachers who benefit from the new collegiality and shared purpose, support, and responsibility.

WHAT I HAVE LEARNED

Over the course of the past seven years, I have worked with thousands of teachers in large urban and small rural schools throughout the United States. While my confidence, excitement, and motivation about curriculum mapping continues to grow, I acknowledge that it is a multilayered, complex journey. I have learned, at times the hard way, the factors that influence the successful implementation of curriculum mapping.

Before beginning the curriculum mapping process, it is vital to examine the history, culture, and climate of a district, including teacher and administrator fear of change and the ever-pressing lack of time. Combining the strong support of administration with shared leadership among teachers is essential for success. Flexibility and patience further impact the degree to which curriculum mapping thrives. In addition, as a result of working with many school districts at various times during the mapping process, I've learned that curriculum mapping can be more easily implemented with the expertise and objectivity of external assistance. A knowledgeable, experienced curriculum mapping expert can provide vital training, if not to the entire staff, then to those leading the initiative. Guidance at the beginning, and support during the curriculum mapping process, will serve to be a wise and time-saving choice.

Curriculum mapping goes far beyond creating a set of maps. The process itself has far-reaching implications for building healthy school environments. Curriculum mapping creates an environment for collaboration, reflection on practice, and discussion of individual and collective belief systems about teaching and learning. Curriculum mapping also provides the authentic process data sorely needed in this age of accountability, high-stakes exams, and federal legislation. This process respects the knowledge and expertise of teachers and serves to elevate the teaching profession.

THE DESIGN OF THE BOOK

This book is designed to assist teachers, curriculum leaders, and administrators in the process of curriculum mapping. While presenting the strengths and challenges associated with curriculum mapping, I offer strategies for addressing the challenges, detailed curriculum mapping steps, teacher stories and anecdotal comments, and implementation forms and templates. These tools can help any district embarking upon this most rewarding and meaningful journey.

STRUCTURAL OVERVIEW OF THE BOOK

Chapter 1: Making the Case for Curriculum Mapping

This chapter provides the research base for curriculum mapping and the ways the process builds collaboration, encourages reflective thought, explores the shared vision of teaching and learning, and focuses on student learning. It includes an examination of the reasons why curriculum mapping is superior to other curriculum models and connects to other school initiatives.

Chapter 2: Before You Begin: What Is Necessary

Building a foundation before beginning curriculum mapping is the focus of Chapter 2. Strategies for setting the stage, building shared leadership, finding the necessary time, and establishing an implementation plan are presented. Questions and surveys are offered that assist educators in receiving valuable baseline information from staff members before implementing curriculum mapping.

Chapter 3: The Curriculum Mapping Process: The Initial Cycle

Chapter 3 offers a detailed description of each step of the initial curriculum mapping cycle. Templates, suggestions for implementation, and teacher stories are presented to assist those leading the initiative to understand the step-by-step process of the initial cycle of curriculum mapping.

Chapter 4: Implementing the Action Plan and Beyond

How to use the maps beyond the initial curriculum mapping cycle is the focus of Chapter 4. Strategies for establishing a communication system, revising and modifying existing maps, and using curriculum mapping data to direct staff development opportunities complete this chapter.

Chapter 5: Curriculum Mapping Software

Choosing a curriculum mapping software program to better facilitate the curriculum mapping process is the emphasis of this chapter. A checklist of criteria to consider when choosing a particular software program and descriptions of the most common curriculum mapping software products are offered.

Conclusion

The last chapter offers final thoughts and reflections about the book and presents future directions for curriculum mapping.

Appendix

The appendix includes a variety of curriculum map samples.

Making the Case for Curriculum Mapping

For if you continue to do what you've always done, you'll always get what you've always got.

—Roland Barth (2001, p. 22)

If improving student learning and student achievement are the goals of our schools, then it is imperative that we examine the processes that influence those goals. Specifically, we must examine how educators plan and implement curriculum and instruction.

WHY CURRICULUM MAPPING IS A BETTER ALTERNATIVE TO OTHER CURRICULUM MODELS

The curriculum models that exist in many schools are based on outdated models that do not reflect the reality that occurs in classrooms. In most schools, curriculum development consists of a process where representative teachers are assigned to curriculum committees to write curriculum based on what they believe should be covered, personal choices, textbooks, favorite lessons, standards, and, all too often, best guesses. The results are often inflexible documents that do not address the ever-changing curricular needs of school districts. The large impressive curriculum binder is photocopied and distributed to the staff and administration; it represents a group's best intentions of what they believe should be taught. However, in reality this document has little connection to real classroom practice. It is usually at this point that the large compilation of well-meaning information is promptly filed somewhere in classrooms and administration offices, not to be looked at again until the next curriculum revision cycle, reinforcing the notion that the curriculum is "finished."

This type of curriculum writing is externally driven and cumbersome to use. It is based on a representative group of teachers' best intentions, not the current curriculum information from all teachers, and seldom reflects the reality of what occurs in classrooms. This is a risky practice in our world of high stakes account-ability inside and outside the school environment. All stakeholders, including those outside the school community, are much more involved and interested in what is being taught in our schools. This was very evident in an incident that occurred in an elementary school prior to the beginning of the school year. The following is the elementary building principal's story of being confronted with a curriculum request from a parent.

When she arrived in his office, the mother explained that she and her husband had just taken jobs in the larger neighboring city, but they were choosing to live in one of the small suburban towns nearby and she was visiting various schools in the area to determine which school would best fit the needs of her son. She went on to describe her son's high interest and aptitude in science. In the course of the conversation, she asked to see the fourth grade science curriculum, as the strength of the science curriculum would help her to decide which school district would be the best for her child. Somewhat surprised, he agreed and took the large science curriculum binder from the shelf (after incon-spicuously brushing the dust off) and showed her the fourth grade sci-ence curriculum, secretly hoping that it was somewhere close to what was actually taught. He really didn't know.

As he later described this parent visit, he shared how much more accurate and professional it would have been to be able to go to his computer and pull up the fourth grade science maps and know with a degree of certainty that this was the current science curriculum taught in his school. What he showed this parent was guesswork.

As parents become more involved and savvy about school choice and how standards and curriculum are or should be implemented in their child's class-rooms, this kind of episode will be the norm rather than the exception.

Another major flaw in many current guides is the lack of assessment infor-mation. There are lists of content, objectives, skills, and standards with no infor-mation about the types of assessment practices that provide the feedback on the achievement of the taught skills. The assessment component of classroom practice is the most important evidence teachers and all stakeholders have to be assured that the content, skills, and standards are taught and mastered by the student.

Curriculum mapping is an alternative that provides a process-oriented model that is respectful of the knowledge of every teacher, encourages collaboration and reflection, and is sensitive to the complexities of student learning and the teaching profession. It offers the flexibility to address the changing curriculum needs of school districts by relying on the active participation and expertise of teachers. It is a process that consists of procedures that include easy curriculum modification, revision, and updates on a timely basis, resulting in a current, reality-based, standards-aligned curriculum.

CURRICULUM MAPPING AND BUILDING EFFECTIVE SCHOOLS

The curriculum maps are valuable documents, in and of themselves, but the process to create and discuss the maps is of equal value. As a district progresses through the curriculum mapping process, they experience the types of activities that build strong, effective schools. The research on effective schools based on the work of Rick DuFour and R. Eaker's (1998) *Professional Learning Communities at Work,* Peter Senge's (2000) *Schools That Learn*, Michael Fullan's (2001) *Leading in the Culture of Change,* Tom Guskey's (2000) *Evaluating Professional Development,* and Roland Barth's (2001) *Learning by Heart* share common tenets. These common practices evident in effective schools include collaboration, reflective inquiry, shared purpose, teacher and student learning, and program coherence. These tenets influence school improvement and are deeply embedded in the curriculum mapping process and outcomes.

Collaboration

True collaboration occurs when all teachers participate in active, meaningful dialogue about teaching practice. Few schools have effective communication systems in place that provide the structure and time for teachers to share and discuss their work. Most schools inherently contain a variety of structural and cultural barriers that prevent teachers from sharing teaching information and from having opportunities to act upon this information in meaningful ways (Fullan, 2001). The expertise and knowledge of teachers is vitally important to teaching and improved student learning. The very foundation of curriculum mapping requires teachers to talk together about what they teach. These conversations compel teachers to analyze practice, make decisions about curriculum changes and modifications, examine assessments, and ultimately learn from each other in a collaborative manner. As these conversations occur, it becomes apparent that the students become the central focus. No longer is it possible to consider what occurs in individual teachers' classrooms as isolated events disjointed from others who are part of the same school system, assessment structure, and who share the same students. Curriculum mapping creates an atmosphere of joint responsibility where all teachers believe that all students are our students. Edward Joyner (2000) offers the following insight, which reinforces the need for collaboration among teachers.

> All too often, there is little communication across grade levels and across content areas. A child gets an experience in one year that might not relate to the next year's experience. . . . [Y]ou have to get agreement among all the teachers about where the starting level for students exists and how fast to carry them along the development path. Teachers in successive grades need to think of themselves as relay racers. Passing a baton. Year after year, as students change and state requirements shift, teachers need to discuss openly the work that is going well, the work that is not, and the changes they need to make. (p. 394)

Curriculum mapping provides a forum for this method of sharing information in a collaborative manner to improve the learning environment for all students.

Reflective Inquiry

Reflecting about teaching practice, both individually and with others, helps all teachers find meaning in their collective experiences, clarify actions, and gain alternative perspectives about teaching practice. In the curriculum mapping process, reflection occurs on an individual basis as one documents the content, skills, and assessments that are taught each month. Shared reflection occurs when teachers have the opportunity to look at one another's maps, reflect upon them, collaboratively discuss questions and new learnings, and, consequently, create a plan of action based on this teacher-generated data. This powerful reflective practice helps teachers create and revise the real curriculum and make data-informed decisions to improve teaching practice and student learning.

Shared Purpose

As teachers come together to discuss the curriculum maps, opportunities arise for teachers to explore the individual and collective value and belief systems within a grade level, school, and ultimately the district. It is often discovered that much of the curriculum is inconsistent, not aligned to standards, repetitive, and based on the desire of the individual teacher. When teachers discuss their maps, they have the opportunity to analyze not only what they are doing but also why they are teaching a subject in a certain way, at a certain time, or including it in the curriculum at all. These professional conversations provide opportunities for teachers to explore their individual vision of teaching and learn about others' viewpoints and the manner in which those personal teaching philosophies meld with the large landscape of teaching and learning for all children.

Student Learning

Curriculum should be based on the best interests and needs of students. However, far too often the curriculum is based on teacher choices and preferences. Placing students in the center of curriculum reform is a vital underpinning of curriculum mapping. Teachers must continually ask themselves if what they are choosing to teach is in the best interest of the students, and how it relates to and connects with what happens to students beyond the scope of the individual classroom. As every teacher analyzes the collective, authentic curriculum data from all teachers and uses this information as a vehicle for making positive, effective changes in the students' learning environment, improved student learning will occur. Furthermore, sharing the maps with students informs them of their journey, sparks their curiosity, and increases their motivation.

Program Coherence

Effective curriculum can become the school's living document that describes the content, skills, and assessment both horizontally within a grade level and/or content area and vertically across grade levels. Current, reality-based dynamic curriculum maps represent a program's consistency and coherence. Process-oriented curriculum mapping helps us make sense of our teaching actions and provides the picture for all stakeholders.

These tenets come together when teachers create, analyze their own and others' maps, are given multiple opportunities to collaborate, reflect about their practice, are cognizant of their vision of education, and, most important, are sensitive to the needs of students.

CONNECTING MAPPING TO OTHER INITIATIVES

Curriculum mapping is not a separate set of tasks to be completed in isolation from other school initiatives but rather serves as the interactive center for the processes and dynamics of school improvement. As teachers and administrators face school improvement initiatives such as higher accountability, standards alignment, curriculum integration, and assessment issues, the curriculum maps become valuable tools to help build the capacity for meaningful change and improvement. Curriculum mapping is a process that engages all staff in curriculum reform and development.

Accountability: Data and Curriculum Go Hand in Hand

According to Fox (2001), there are three main sources of school data: outcome, demographic, and process. The outcome data is comprised of student achievement data, attendance data, behavior records, and other types of survey or satisfaction measures. The demographic data represent student population characteristics that include race, ethnicity, economic level, disability status, and limited English proficiency. The third type of data is process data, which include the curriculum that guides classroom instruction.

In recent years many school districts have organized data analysis events, often called data retreats, where teachers and administrators come together to unpack the outcome and demographic data to determine achievement patterns, student patterns, and patterns of program quality (Sargent, 2000). While all data reflects the challenges that face our schools, the process data is the main source of data that schools can significantly control through curriculum and instructional strategy modification and revision. Curriculum mapping and curriculum maps provide a critical process-oriented data source. Data analysis and curriculum mapping must be tandem events, one informing the other. Bringing together the results of data analysis and using that information to impact the action piece, the curriculum, allows teachers to see the big picture of the school's accountability system and to make effective changes. Curriculum mapping is an integral part of a school's accountability system.

Implications of No Child Left Behind

The spirit of No Child Left Behind legislation is to improve the public education system and increase student achievement. This legislation is designed to improve school outcomes by making strong connections between standards and curriculum, especially in reading and mathematics. If schools are to make these connections, it is imperative that an effective standards and curriculum alignment process be in place.

Standards Alignment

Academic standards have become the consensus statements for what school children in the United States should know and be able to do. The standards provide the structural framework for the written curriculum, requiring a close alignment between standards and curriculum. Facilitating the alignment process has proven to be a challenging, lengthy, and often ineffective process. Teachers have struggled to translate standards language into meaningful curriculum largely because current methods of standards analysis have been difficult and time consuming to realize.

The following is an example of how the standards analysis and curriculum alignment process has typically occurred.

> The standards alignment process began with a large representative group of teachers who met for a three-day workshop during the summer. These teachers brought curricular materials consisting of large curriculum binders, textbooks, and various other curriculum guides along with the most recent copy of the state standards. To document standards and curriculum alignment, representative groups of teachers would examine each written standard, discuss what they believed it meant, and identify the extent to which they believed the standard was covered, not covered, or questionably covered. The discussion would include consulting the curriculum guide or textbook to determine if the standard was listed, or in some cases, one of the teachers, as a representative of the grade level or content area, would indicate that the teachers in his or her respective team or grade level do or do not "cover" that specific standard. When consensus was reached, a group member would check the appropriate box on the provided standards alignment form. At the end of the workshop, there were pages of completed standards checklists representing the faulty belief that the district's curriculum was "aligned."

This type of alignment process raises the questions, Aligned to what? Aligned to a document that no one uses, a textbook that is outdated and soon to be replaced, or based on the representative voice of a teacher with little or no authentic knowledge of what occurs in the classrooms of his or her colleagues? Accurate alignment must begin with knowledge of the curriculum that is actually taught. Someone's best guess will not create an accurate alignment. The alignment should also contain some type of standards analysis so everyone understands the jargon-heavy standards language.

Furthermore, to authentically determine standards and curriculum alignment, there must be a discussion of the types of assessments that provide feedback regarding the extent to which students have mastered the content and skills reflective of the standards. Merely stating that it is "covered" in the curriculum is not enough.

Curriculum mapping helps teachers to analyze the standards language and to meaningfully align the currently taught content, skills, and implemented assessments to the standards. The curriculum mapping process provides a forum for all teachers to discuss this analysis with their colleagues. This analysis, reflection, and collaboration helps teachers arrive at new understandings about what the standards truly mean for themselves, and their students, both vertically and horizontally, and then to meaningfully align the standards to the authentic curriculum.

As one classroom teacher who was mapping her curriculum and aligning what she taught to the standards stated:

> It's when I got to the standards alignment part that mapping began to make sense. I thought I knew the standards, but until I really had to compare them to what I actually do did I understand them. I could now see that what I do is part of a bigger system; that's when it made sense to me. (Elementary teacher, personal communication, January 2004)

The Literacy Connection

A major component of No Child Left Behind legislation and a strong indicator of student success is literacy competency. To meet this challenge, all teachers must understand literacy processes and integrate those processes across all curricular areas. In short, to some extent, all teachers must become literacy teachers. These cross-curricular literacy strategies, which will be addressed in Chapter 4, include examining text structure and format, editing and revising written work, using common writing rubrics, incorporating nonfiction and fiction texts, including oral communication skills, and enhancing and intensifying vocabulary development. No longer should any student believe that literacy skills are only relevant in English class. Focusing on literacy skills across the curriculum makes them a districtwide priority. Teachers can begin to identify common literacy-based skills that must cross all content areas. All teachers can design common literacy-based assessments that enhance all curriculum areas.

As teachers engage in professional conversations about maps, cross-curricular information is shared that can provide literacy instructional strategies to those teachers who feel less competent about their own literacy skills. Curricular conversations provide informal professional development.

New Teachers and Veteran Teachers

When most new teachers begin their teaching career, they are overwhelmed with feelings of uncertainty. Having very little or inadequate curriculum materials further complicates the already challenging life of a first-year teacher. Invariably, when curriculum mapping is presented to faculties, some teachers express the positive impact a current, easily understood curriculum would have had on the effectiveness of their first year of teaching. While not completely eliminating the anxieties of a first-year teacher, having easy access to current curriculum maps from current colleagues and/or the prior course or classroom teacher greatly assists classroom teaching and, more important, positively impacts student learning. In addition, as new teachers and their mentors collaborate on curriculum maps, the process promotes collegiality and reflection, further strengthening the mentor/mentee relationship (Udelhofen & Larson, 2003).

On the other end of the spectrum, those teachers who are close to retirement have a powerful role in curriculum mapping. It is vital that our most honored colleagues have a vehicle to leave their teaching legacy. Upon retirement, these experts in their field too often take with them an enormous collection of curriculum experience. This wealth of knowledge is lost to new teachers, remaining colleagues, students, and the teaching profession. Curriculum maps provide a process and product to share years of teaching knowledge and experience to benefit teachers and students alike.

Developing Professional Learning Communities

According to Roland Barth (2001), a professional learning community is a place where teachers and students care about, look after, root for one another, and work together for the good of the whole, in times of need as well as times of celebration. As teachers come together to assimilate new ideas and teaching practices, discuss what is and is not working in their own teaching, and develop ways to modify and improve the real curriculum—all steps inherent in the curriculum mapping process—professional learning communities are created. A collaborative culture is created that builds results-oriented environments that offer the best hope for transforming schools and energizing teachers to better meet student needs.

Curriculum mapping is a process-oriented curriculum development model that builds environments that offer great hope for transforming schools and energizing teachers to better meet student needs. As in any worthwhile endeavor, it is time-intensive, and there are foundational strategies to be considered before embarking on this initiative. It is a process that produces a clear road map for instructional content for the whole school. However, the process is much more beneficial than its name suggests, as it also builds learning communities, maintains focus on the goals of No Child Left Behind, grounds conversations about student data, and promotes the sharing and transfer of teacher knowledge and expertise. Chapter 2 presents important steps to consider before beginning the formal curriculum mapping process.

Before You Begin

What Is Necessary

What we know from practice is that adults learn best when they're interested, feel connected with the topic, feel supported through the learning process and are able to implement what they've learned.

—Pamela Nevills (2003, p. 20)

In itself, curriculum mapping is a relatively simple concept. However, implementing curriculum mapping is a multifaceted process that requires changes in teacher attitudes, perceptions, and actions. It is a long-term commitment that benefits from forethought and planning before it is formally introduced to the faculty. This chapter presents strategies for building a solid foundation when initiating curriculum mapping.

CURRICULUM MAPPING: A SHIFT IN PERCEPTION

Curriculum mapping requires a shift in how curriculum is perceived, developed, and practiced, which requires a shift in thinking on two major fronts. First, each individual teacher's curriculum becomes public. Curriculum is no longer an action that occurs in isolation based on teachers' desires, but rather it becomes meaningful information that is shared with colleagues as an interactive tool to improve student learning. It is no longer a series of individually owned activities, materials, and projects. Traditionally, teachers have been accustomed to "guarding" their individual lessons, projects, and assessment strategies. For example, one teacher expressed the following sentiment:

I probably shouldn't say this, but I've worked long hard hours after school and weekends to develop my materials while others are coming in at 8:00 and going home at 3:30. Why should I share all of my materials with them?

While this sentiment has fairness on its side, it does not benefit students. This perception of ownership and privatization of curriculum is far too common.

The second shift in thinking is that the curriculum is a dynamic, ever-changing, continuous process—not a finished product. The best teachers have always updated their curriculum; the schools need to do the same. Just as our students, our society, and our world change on a continual basis, so must the content of the curriculum. The traditional "finished" curriculum binders that remain dormant for years at a time make it nearly impossible to modify or change any portion of these documents in a timely and efficient manner.

These shifts should be acknowledged and addressed throughout the introductory stages of the curriculum mapping process as the key players in this process explore their rationale for considering this curriculum development model.

WHY ARE WE DOING THIS?

The interest in curriculum mapping commonly emerges from a variety of sources. An administrator or teacher may have attended a curriculum mapping presentation, or possibly a neighboring district is involved with mapping the curriculum. For some it is in response to external pressure to update and align curriculum to academic standards. Others may be looking for a way to strengthen the curriculum to increase test scores. While all of these reasons are valid, they usually aren't enough to successfully begin the process with an entire teaching staff. Because of the complexities associated with curriculum mapping, it is wise for school leadership teams to consider key questions before embarking on the curriculum mapping process and presenting it to the teaching staff. The questions proposed in Figure 2.1 present key discussion questions to explore as you begin curriculum mapping.

After looking closely at the questions on page 11 and determining the reasons for pursuing curriculum mapping, the next step is to bring together a districtwide, representative group of educators to learn more about the process.

SETTING THE STAGE: HEADS-UP MEETING

Creating the foundation for developing curriculum mapping will require the support and work of the teaching staff. Although the educators who are spearheading this initiative will understand that the long-term benefits of curriculum mapping far outweigh the challenges, these benefits are not usually initially apparent to all teachers. Far too often, curriculum mapping appears as another top-down mandate. For that reason, it is vital that the teachers, those who will be most directly involved with the process and will heavily invest their time in it,

Figure 2.1   Questions to Consider Before Beginning the Curriculum Mapping
Process

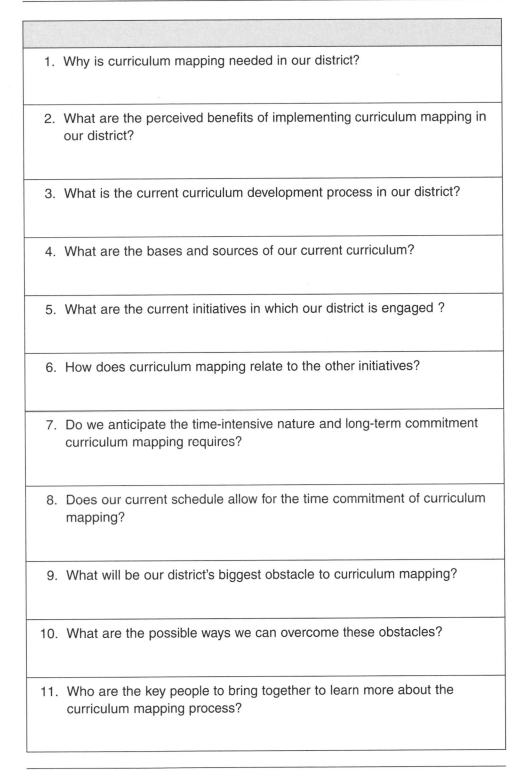

1. Why is curriculum mapping needed in our district?

2. What are the perceived benefits of implementing curriculum mapping in our district?

3. What is the current curriculum development process in our district?

4. What are the bases and sources of our current curriculum?

5. What are the current initiatives in which our district is engaged ?

6. How does curriculum mapping relate to the other initiatives?

7. Do we anticipate the time-intensive nature and long-term commitment curriculum mapping requires?

8. Does our current schedule allow for the time commitment of curriculum mapping?

9. What will be our district's biggest obstacle to curriculum mapping?

10. What are the possible ways we can overcome these obstacles?

11. Who are the key people to bring together to learn more about the curriculum mapping process?

be involved with the decision to begin this initiative. Teachers will better accept any new initiative when they can internalize the process and make it part of their reality. Any successful initiative must be connected to the teachers' aspirations and the needs of and benefits for the school system (Senge, 2000).

A heads-up meeting should be planned for a broad group of stakeholders. At this meeting, the leadership team, including internal or external facilitators, introduce the curriculum mapping process to explain why it is being considered and to provide a forum for open conversations where attitudes and questions are examined. The stakeholders at this meeting include representative classroom teachers from all levels and/or content areas, curriculum personnel, special education teachers, related arts teachers, support service representatives, administrators, and school board representation. If possible, invite a curriculum mapping expert to present the process and answer questions. This may be a consultant or colleague from another district who has successfully implemented curriculum mapping. Be prepared to discuss the following agenda items:

- An introduction to curriculum mapping that includes
  - The benefits of curriculum mapping and why it is being considered
    - The Curriculum Questionnaire for Teachers (Figure 2.2) may be distributed to participants to help analyze the district's current curriculum.
  - An explanation of the time commitment, effort, diligence, ongoing support, and encouragement curriculum mapping requires
  - A clear commitment from administration to complete the process. Administrators should reaffirm that they are partners with teachers in this process.

- An introduction to the curriculum mapping process
  - Samples of curriculum maps
  - Preliminary implementation plans for Year 1, 2, and 3
  - Options for completing the process

- Exploration of the current district issues and concerns that may impede the curriculum mapping process
- Ample time for questions and answers
- An introduction to the curriculum mapping software programs

This is the first step in establishing a schoolwide power base of support for the process of curriculum mapping.

BUILDING SHARED LEADERSHIP: STEERING COMMITTEE TO OVERSEE THE PROCESS

Districts that have experienced the highest success rate with curriculum mapping have highly visible, engaged leadership at all levels. No one person can lead this work. There must be a collective understanding of the value and

Figure 2.2   Curriculum Questionnaire for Teachers

Is the curriculum our district currently uses to guide instruction:	Yes	Somewhat	No
1. highly visible and easily accessible to teachers, students, and parents?			
2. presented in a user-friendly format that is easy to read and understand?			
3. easily and continually revised on a timely (at least yearly) basis—based on teacher input, student results, collaboration, and latest research: *I never have to ask "What happened to the curriculum work we did last year?"*			
4. a tool that provides every teacher with real, current information about the content, skills, and assessments that all teachers are actually teaching in our district?			
5. a tool that is easy to use for teachers who are now to teaching or new to the district?			
6. clearly based on student learning and achievement rather than teacher choice?			
7. a tool that provides specific information about the content and skills that precede and follow a particular grade level or course: *I am never frustrated, because the unit I planned had already been taught to my students.*			
8. at the core of teaching practice?			
9. clearly embedded in district and state standards?			
Other questions and/or comments:			

outcomes, with representation and leadership from a variety of stakeholder groups. The success of any initiative depends upon an environment where principals and teachers work together mobilized by care, common goals, and mutual respect to develop and nurture shared expertise (Fullan, 2001). Collaborative leadership is what sustains team effort far beyond the tenure of a single leader and will last. It is important that a committee of key stakeholders be established to build an internal commitment where their ideas and intrinsic motivation can help to activate the support and positive action of the entire faculty. The members of this group can become the leadership base that will prove to be invaluable as teachers learn the curriculum mapping process. See the Steering Committee Planning Template (Figure 2.3) to help organize the steering committee. The composition, roles, and responsibilities of this group are as follows:

Group Composition:

- Representatives from each grade level and content area
- Teachers who are knowledgeable of the curriculum mapping process and believe in its merits
- Representatives who are highly respected by colleagues
- Union representation
- Representatives who are willing to act as on-site "go-to" contacts to be available to colleagues to answer questions and help facilitate the curriculum mapping process
- Representatives who will set a positive tone with their colleagues regarding the importance and benefits of curriculum mapping

Group Roles and Responsibilities:

- To complete maps prior to introducing curriculum mapping to the staff
- To assist teachers to recognize the value of the process and how it connects to other schoolwide initiatives
- To exercise positive pressure on teachers to meet deadlines for completing their maps
- To identify what the outcomes/indicators of success will be
- To mobilize others to believe in the process
- To provide support as needed
- To cheerlead and celebrate the ongoing efforts and successes of the individuals and teams

If curriculum mapping is to be continued and sustained over time, it must become part of the fabric of the district, led by teachers and administrators alike who share an investment in the process.

ESTABLISHING AN IMPLEMENTATION PLAN

Finding the time is consistently one of the largest issues raised by teachers when introduced to the curriculum mapping process. Teachers have incredibly busy

Figure 2.3   Steering Committee Planning Template

	Name	Building	Position	Content Area and/or Grade Level
Teacher Representatives:				
Union Representative:				
Administrators:				
School Board Representative:				

schedules, and the challenge to find adequate time in already overextended schedules is daunting. It is vital that those organizing the curriculum mapping process estimate the time each step will take and create an implementation plan that outlines when and how each step will be completed. This type of forethought and planning helps to make the initiative credible to the teaching staff and provides substance and organization to the process. Figure 2.4 presents a planning template that lists each step and the estimated time that each step of the initial curriculum mapping cycle requires. The details of each step are explained in depth in Chapter 3.

While the time allotted may seem optimistically short, teachers should be encouraged that while their mapping efforts should not be superficial, they also should not include more than is necessary. The first map may require more than the suggested time as teachers are learning a new skill. However, after the first map is completed, teachers very often find that subsequent maps are easier and not as time consuming to complete.

STRATEGIES FOR FINDING THE TIME

There is no school district that enjoys an overabundance of free time. This time shortage requires a close examination of the current ways time is being spent and an exploration of creative ways to reallocate and revise the existing time structures. The steps in curriculum mapping require teachers to have independent work time to create and edit maps and also to have time to meet with colleagues in small and large groups. There are a variety of ways to release teachers on an individual basis as well as to provide time for small and large group meetings. Those strategies include the following:

- Sharing students: combining two or more classes for a joint activity, thereby freeing up an individual teacher or small group of teachers
- Asking teaching assistants or parent volunteers to supervise noninstructional activities
  - Extended lunchtime
  - Videos
  - Field trips

- Hiring floating substitute teachers to free teachers for specific blocks of time
- Planning school assemblies that all teachers do not need to attend
- Exploring inservice days and staff meeting time.
- Using common prep/planning time
- Scheduling all students in special classes at the same time, which can free general education teachers to work in small groups
- Scheduling the principal, assistant principal, or curriculum director to take over class supervision
- Banking time: Adding 5–10 minutes of instructional time per day to enable extra staff development days
- Adjusting start and end time
  - Late starts
  - Early dismissals

Figure 2.4   Suggested Timetable Worksheet

Curriculum Mapping Steps *The First Cycle of Mapping*	Strategy for Allocating Time to Complete This Step	Date to Be Completed
Step 1: COMPLETING INDIVIDUAL MAPS This step is completed independently by each teacher *Time Needed:* To map out the content, skills, and assessments for one content area or prep for an entire school year will take 4–5 hours. K–2 language arts will take somewhat longer.		
STEP 2: REVIEWING GROUPS OF MAPS This step is completed independently by each teacher. Each teacher reads a set of completed maps using a recording sheet to document findings. *Time Needed:* This phase takes about 3–4 hours depending upon how many maps each teacher will edit. Usually teachers begin by editing 12–14 maps within and across grade levels and content areas.		
STEP 3: SHARING THE REVIEWS IN SMALL GROUPS The initial small group review occurs at each site. This phase requires small groups of teachers (7–8) to gather together and discuss the edits. *Time Needed:* This step takes approximately 2 hours and requires small groups of teachers to meet.		
STEP 4: REPORTING THE SMALL GROUP RESULTS TO ALL FACULTY This step requires the faculty at each site to meet together to report the findings from the small group review. *Time Needed:* This phase is usually 2–3 hours.		
STEP FIVE: DEVELOPING AN ACTION PLAN Decisions are made by grade level or building to address the issues presented in the previous large group reporting step and a plan is developed to address the concerns. *Time Needed:* 1–2 hours planning time.		

MAKING PRELIMINARY DECISIONS
BEFORE YOU BEGIN BACKWARD
OR FORWARD MAPPING

As teachers create their curriculum maps, there are two processes for collecting the curriculum data: backward or forward mapping. These are sometimes referred to as journal or projection mapping. (The details for collecting the curriculum data are presented in Chapter 3.) Forward mapping requires teachers to record their planned content, skills, and assessments for the entire school year at one time. Blocks of time will need to be scheduled for teachers to complete their year-long curriculum maps. Backward mapping asks teachers to document the content, skills, and assessments at the end of each month as they are taught. Time is allocated each month for teachers to record the content, skills, and assessments that were taught that particular month.

Some districts may choose to implement a combination of both strategies to complete a year-long map. For example, if a district begins the mapping process in midyear and wishes to map the entire year at one time, this would require recalling what had been taught in the months prior to beginning mapping, a type of backward mapping, and also forward mapping as one projects what will be taught in the remaining months.

Making the decision as to which approach to take will depend upon the available time to map and, in some cases, the preferences of the teachers. It doesn't matter which approach is chosen, as the end result is the same: a current, authentic map of what is taught. See Figure 2.5 for a comparison of backward and forward mapping.

Do We Map All Content Areas
and/or Courses at the Beginning?

Deciding which content areas and how many preps will be mapped initially are also decisions to be made at the beginning of the process. Districts that are creating projection maps often elect to require elementary staff to begin with one or two content areas and content-specific teachers at the middle and high school level to map two preps. The focus should be on the core courses rather than electives. All elective courses will be mapped, but during the first cycle, it is recommended to begin with the core, required courses. Districts that are journal mapping often require that all content areas and preps be mapped each month. These decisions again are based on the allocated time and the preferences of the teachers. Keep in mind that the goal is to have all courses and all content areas mapped, and it doesn't matter which approach is implemented. It is important to consider that at the middle and high school level, it will be difficult to proceed with subsequent curriculum mapping steps until all core courses are mapped.

When and How Should Special
Education and Support Services Teachers Map?

All special education teachers need to complete curriculum maps, but the format of the maps may vary according to the configuration of the special education

Figure 2.5   Backward (Journal) Mapping Versus Forward (Projection) Mapping

Initial Mapping Format	Advantages	Disadvantages
Backward Mapping (*Sometimes referred to as journal or diary mapping*)	• Is not as time-intensive at the beginning, as it will require a small amount of time each month to record the content, skills, and assessments taught that particular month. • Possibly allows for a more accurate account of what was actually taught.	• It slows the completion of the initial mapping cycle, as teachers cannot proceed to the editing step until maps are completed, which is at the end of the academic year. The next steps would most likely not occur until the beginning of the next school year. • The curriculum mapping process can lose momentum • Monthly check-ins must occur with each teacher to keep abreast of each teacher's progress.
Forward Mapping (*Sometimes referred to as projection mapping*)	• The initial curriculum maps are completed within a short time frame, enabling teachers to move to the next steps of mapping much faster. It is conceivable that if a district allocates the appropriate amount of time, the initial cycle of mapping can be completed in one academic year.	• It is time-intensive at the beginning. • Some teachers have difficulty projecting future teaching or recalling what they taught in prior months. This may especially be an issue for those teachers who do not keep a plan book.

program. Most often the type of special education program, inclusionary model or self-contained model, dictates the format of the special education maps.

Regardless of the model, it is recommended that the special education teachers complete their maps after the general education teachers have completed their maps. As they read the general educator's content, skills, and assessments, they are better able to create modified versions of those maps reflecting the changes they make in their curriculum to meet the needs of their special education students. These modifications may include focusing on the essential skills but requiring mastery at different levels or implementing alternative assessment measures more appropriate for their students. The changes can be made on the general education teacher's map by highlighting, color coding, and/or underlining the modifications and then saving the map as the special education teacher's own map. This way the special education teacher will have a map for each student but will not have to create a map for each student from the beginning. Also, some special education teachers may find it beneficial to look at the general education teachers' maps that match the learning level of the special education student. For example, if the fourth grade special education student is functioning at a second grade level, the teacher may want to look at the second grade general education curriculum maps.

Some special education teachers elect to create maps that complement the individualized education plan (IEP) established for their students, and the maps are attached to the IEP.

Special education teachers who teach very low-functioning students may choose to map by semester or year rather than by month. Those maps include basic content, skills, and assessments. Again, this will be largely dependent upon the context of the classroom.

Those teachers who are part of student support services such as speech and language teachers and school psychologists can also create modified versions of the general education and/or special education maps, depending upon the students they serve. The bottom line is that all teachers create curriculum maps reflective of what is taught.

As general education, special education, and support services teachers share their maps, communication is greatly enhanced, which provides tremendous learning opportunities for teachers and, most important, their students.

Establishing a Timeline for Implementation

All of these decisions need to be made and an appropriate timeline established before a district begins mapping. The following is one example of how a district established a plan for finding the time to implement curriculum mapping.

This small, rural school district had very little current curricular information and had spent a number of months exploring various curriculum development processes. When I was hired to work with the district, the media specialist/curriculum leader, a small group of teachers, and the district superintendent/principal had decided that curriculum mapping was the curriculum development process they were most interested in. We worked together to organize an initial afterschool heads-up meeting with interested staff members. Following this meeting and the teachers' cautious, positive feedback, the committee decided to proceed with curriculum mapping. The next step was to develop a step-by-step implementation plan. The planning committee knew they would have to develop strategies to release teachers for all curriculum mapping work, and these strategies would have to be presented to the school board. The initial plan asked for two early-release days per month, far exceeding the routine practice of two release days per semester. This schedule would require additional minutes added to each day to make up this early-release time. Because early-release time was not viewed favorably within the community, there was great trepidation about presenting this plan to the board. The school board presentation clearly outlined the benefits of this curricular work and the high need for a more meaningful, standards-aligned curriculum. The presentation also included a clear long-term commitment from administration and teachers. The committee believed that if the required time could not be established, it would not be possible to implement curriculum mapping.

See Figure 2.6 for the established timeline that was presented to the board.

Much to the amazement and relief of the planning committee, the plan was accepted. What is remarkable about this achievement is that this scheduling change was a major shift in how the school year was organized. It was evident that sound planning, support from a wide array of stakeholder groups, and a clear explanation of the benefits of this process made a solid case for implementing this curriculum development initiative.

CURRICULUM MAPPING TRAINING

As a result of preliminary planning meetings and training, there may be a number of teachers familiar with curriculum mapping. These teachers will serve to support and encourage others as they learn the process, but it is recommended that they not facilitate curriculum mapping training. Unless indistrict staff leaders are very knowledgeable and experienced with the curriculum mapping process, it is more effective to have an outside curriculum mapping expert provide the training. During initial training sessions, a wide variety of questions and concerns will surface that an experienced facilitator will be better able to address. Furthermore, it is very important that all faculty members receive a clear, consistent, step-by-step introduction to the curriculum mapping process. If this does not occur, there is the risk that teachers and administrators will receive inconsistent messages that will be confusing and frustrating as they begin to complete their maps.

USING TECHNOLOGY

Many districts begin by using a simple computer-generated template. However, it is strongly encouraged that schools explore curriculum mapping software programs. Curriculum mapping software programs assist teachers to more easily and efficiently enter curriculum information, make adjustments, examine colleagues' maps, perform searches, align standards, and use the Internet to expand mapping capabilities (Jacobs, 2003). This topic is covered in more detail in Chapter 5.

Figure 2.6 Curriculum Mapping Timetable

Process	Dates	Participants	Funding	Results
Curriculum mapping training, including curriculum mapping software training	June 8, 9, 10	Teacher and administrator volunteers / Outside consultant	Teachers were paid extended contract money	A core group of teacher leaders trained / Math and language arts maps completed by core groups
Curriculum mapping training, including curriculum mapping software training	August 30 & 31	All faculty / Outside consultant	Contractual inservice days prior to the beginning of school	Staff trained in curriculum process / Math and language arts maps begun
Assessment inservice	September 2 / One early release half-day	All faculty / Outside consultant	Contractual early release	Teachers more knowledgeable about assessment practices. Will assist teachers as they record assessments on their maps.
Curriculum mapping workday	September 3 / One half-day	All faculty	Contractual early release	Completed curriculum maps
Essential questions inservice	October 13 / One half-day	All faculty / Outside consultant	Contractual early release	Teachers introduced to essential questions to be developed and entered on maps
Curriculum mapping workday	October 14 / One half-day	All faculty	Contractual early release	Completing curriculum maps
Editing curriculum maps	November 16 / One half-day	All faculty	Contractual early release	Edited maps
Small group sharing	December 9 / One half-day	All faculty / Outside consultant	Contractual early release	Small group findings
Large group sharing	January 11 / One half-day	All faculty / Outside consultant	Contractual early release	Large group findings
Developing action plan based on large group results	February 16 / One half-day	All faculty / Outside consultant	Contractual early release	Action plan
Continued action plan work	February 17 / One half-day	All staff	Contractual early release	Action plan
Exploring other district data sources and connecting to mapping	March 10 / One half-day	All staff	Contractual early release	Updated maps
TBA based on curriculum mapping progress	April 19	All staff	Contractual early release	
Curriculum mapping review and plan for next school year	May 12	All staff	Contractual early release	Plan for next school year

BEYOND THE TIME ISSUE: CULTURE, TRUST, AND FLEXIBILITY

Changing one's beliefs, behaviors, and perceptions is a complex endeavor that most often initially results in resistance. Implementing curriculum mapping is no different. While most teachers will not argue the merits of curriculum mapping, they will be apprehensive about documenting and sharing their curriculum with others. The extent to which this will be a problem is dependent upon the climate and culture in the district and how much the faculty trusts one another. Addressing these tacit and explicit fears can mean the success or failure of curriculum mapping.

Trust Factor

Trust is what connects us and must be built before teachers are able to engage in honest, direct, and productive conversations with colleagues about their teaching. Posing difficult questions and gathering feedback from staff at the onset can help those leading this initiative to address possible obstacles before they occur.

One teacher submitted the following concern about curriculum mapping in a staff survey in 2004 prior to implementation:

> I think maybe my biggest concern is the embarrassment of knowing how much I teach is overlapped elsewhere because I haven't taken the time to find out.

If curriculum mapping is to succeed, it is very important that this type of apprehension be addressed and resolved. Leaders need to emphasize that this process is not linked to individual teacher evaluation but to all school improvement, building learning communities, and improving student learning.

Figure 2.7 offers possible discussion questions to bring anxieties to the forefront. These questions can be posed to the initial heads-up meeting participants, steering committee, or other faculty members in other small group settings.

If it is determined as a result of the questions on page 24 that there are issues related to communication and trust, it is advised to allocate additional time to explore these issues before the curriculum mapping process begins. Robert Garmston's norms of collaboration offered in *The Adaptive School* (Garmston & Wellman, 1999) and strategies offered in *Learning by Heart* by Roland Barth (2001) are two possible sources for improving communication skills and school culture issues.

Flexibility

Although curriculum mapping is a step-by-step process, it does not always follow a linear path. It would be nice if all teachers had a complete understanding of the process at the onset and completed their maps at the same time.

Figure 2.7   Faculty Discussion Questions

	Almost Always	Some-times	Rarely	Almost Never	Don't Know	Comments
We acknowledge one another's ideas.						
We are able to respectfully communicate with one another.						
Our staff interacts with caution.						
We believe that we are a good staff that believes in each other and ourselves.						
I am always able to find someone to help me when I need it.						
Our staff cares about each other professionally and personally.						
Our staff is student-centered.						
Our staff is open to new ideas.						
Our staff can openly discuss any concern.						
The teachers on our staff are lifelong learners.						
I feel accepted and not judged by our staff.						

Just as our students learn and progress at different rates, so do our teachers. Some teachers will grasp the idea and complete their maps with relative ease before or within the allocated time frame. Others will require more time, reassurance, and support. Still others will resist the movement at all costs and believe that if they resist long enough, it will go away. Curriculum mapping requires a flexible environment that celebrates the successes, provides additional support as needed, and, in some cases, demands strong accountability measures for those who actively refuse. It will require patience, time, tolerance, appreciation, and commitment. The following excerpt describes one district's initial curriculum mapping experience.

One District's Journey

For nearly a year this K–12 school district had been mapping the curriculum. The previous summer I had facilitated a three-day curriculum mapping training for a group of teacher leaders and all administrators. It was also at this time that a curriculum mapping software program was introduced by the district media specialist. During this three-day training, an implementation plan was established that included staff training and an essential questions workshop. Scheduled time was allocated for every teacher to keep a monthly journal map of each month's content, skills, and assessments using the mapping software. The teachers decided that language arts would be mapped K–12 and teachers who did not teach language arts or math would map two of their respective courses. Principals had agreed that they would allocate a portion of their faculty meeting time along with other planning time for mapping work each month. As the school year progressed, the two K–8 buildings were making relatively good progress while the high school was experiencing difficulties completing its required monthly maps. Lack of sufficient time, software problems, and perhaps misgivings regarding the process itself seemed to be the major issues. Slowing the process for the high school and making other modifications were attempted with mixed results. At the end of the year, a meeting was called to assess the progress of curriculum mapping and to plan for the following school year. As each building reported its progress, it was apparent that the issues at the high school remained. On an individual basis, the high school teachers seemed to understand the merits of curriculum mapping, but as a collective group, there were still obstacles and issues to overcome to make curriculum mapping work as designed. At this point, those leading the initiative were apprehensive that although the K–8 teachers were experiencing positive outcomes, it was not going to work at the high school level. Shortly after this meeting, I had a conversation with my brother-in-law, a former high school teacher, who was now in an administrative role. When I shared my concerns, he very succinctly stated, "They're afraid, and until you get to the basis of their fears, it's not going to work." I took his words to heart and again met with the curriculum team and asked specific questions regarding the high school issues. We took each issue and addressed the concerns and developed a plan to overcome these obstacles and reassure those most ambivalent about the benefits of the process. It further helped that there was teacher and administrator representation from the K–8 building that again reiterated the benefits and successes they were experiencing. Together, we came up with a plan to address the resistance.

1. The principal organized each teacher's course load, and with the help of teachers in each department, organized a list of core classes for each teacher to map first. The principal then scheduled a time for teachers to meet to discuss those curriculums as soon as possible.

2. A system would be facilitated by the high school principal to keep abreast of the status of the maps and provide monthly mapping progress.

3. The software was upgraded to a more user-friendly format, and the computers on the high school teachers' desktops were replaced with newer models that would better accommodate the mapping software.

4. Opportunities for high school teachers to view seventh and eighth grade maps would be facilitated to assist with consistency and continuity between the middle level and high school curriculums.

5. The updated, long-term plan would be shared with all staff to illustrate the big picture of mapping.

Although the high school had not advanced to the stage that we had all hoped, by listening to their fears, modifying the process to better meet their needs, and creating a plan that was supported by the principal and teacher leaders, it increased the likelihood that curriculum mapping would be successful. It was a matter of listening to concerns and being flexible with the process. It also helped to share the success recorded from the other buildings.

This story and the other issues presented in this chapter represent many of the challenges associated with the initial introduction of curriculum mapping and the importance of deliberately spending time examining district-specific issues that may later prove to be obstacles. At the beginning of the process, when teachers are recording the data, it's difficult for most teachers to see the big picture and understand the benefits of their work. It is the role of those leading the charge to continually provide support for the process and a vision of the big picture that includes collegial sharing, clarity of curriculum goals, greater sense of efficacy, participation in a larger effort, and, most important, improved experiences for students.

The Curriculum Mapping Process

The Initial Cycle

Schools that simply adopt canned curriculum programs or allow textbooks to dictate the curriculum make a fundamental mistake. Without collaborative processes that foster ownership in decisions, schools will not generate the shared commitments and results orientation of a learning community. Thus, the process of curriculum development is at least as important as the final product.

—Rick DuFour (1998, p. 153)

This chapter focuses on the steps of curriculum mapping. The process is consistent with the work of Heidi Hayes Jacobs (1997, 2001). It includes modifications from my curriculum mapping consulting experiences and emphasizes core values surfaced by the research on effective schools discussed in Chapter 1, including the importance of collaboration, reflective practice, shared purpose, linkage between teacher and student learning, and program coherence.

THE CURRICULUM MAPPING STEPS

Step 1: Completing individual maps

Step 2: Reviewing groups of maps

Step 3: Sharing the reviews with colleagues

Step 4: Reporting the results of small group work with all faculty

Step 5: Developing an action plan based on faculty findings

Step 6: Implementing the action plan and beyond

When these steps are first presented in an overview to the full faculty, it would be helpful to also share with them the emotions that they may experience at various stages of the process, recognizing and allowing for feelings of frustration at the outset but also previewing the feelings of exhilaration, success, satisfaction, and collegiality that they will experience as the process evolves.

As described in Chapter 2, the process begins after ample time has been allocated to setting the stage. By the time a school, region, or district is ready to start the curriculum mapping steps, all teachers have been introduced to this process, a steering committee is in place, a clear schedule and timeline have been established, and decisions have been made regarding the content areas, courses to be mapped, and map format. Regardless of which format you choose, backward or forward mapping (described in Chapter 2), the directions for the first step remain the same.

This is also the time to offer curriculum mapping training that clearly and consistently presents the process. It is highly recommended that the training be presented to all staff in a clear, consistent manner by a curriculum mapping trainer who is experienced and knowledgeable in the curriculum mapping process.

Using Technology

Purchasing curriculum mapping software is strongly encouraged (this topic is covered in depth in Chapter 5), but if your district is not using a specific program, it is recommended that teachers use a Microsoft Word table or Excel to complete Step 1. Even if a software program is purchased after teachers complete their individual maps, the data can usually be cut and pasted into the curriculum mapping program. Even with available technology, some teachers will want to handwrite their maps, but this is strongly discouraged. The maps will be continually revised and modified, and to handwrite them is like completing a master's thesis on a legal pad of paper. However, if teachers prefer to begin to record their curriculum data on paper and pencil maps to get a better sense of the process, they should then be encouraged to move quickly to electronic format for easy review and adjustment. For some the issue may be slow or inadequate typing skills. If this is the case, find someone in the district to type their maps for them.

Step 1: Creating Individual Maps

The basic data on the curriculum maps includes the content, skills, and assessments for every course that is taught.

Guidelines for Creating the Maps

1. Every teacher collects and records the curriculum data *independently*. The basic premise of curriculum mapping is developing an honest, reality-based, authentic curriculum. This can only occur when each teacher documents what happens in his or her classroom. If teachers work together to create their maps, there is a high likelihood that they will influence one another, thus impacting the authenticity of what goes on the maps. Group dynamics can influence the conversations and consequently skew the data. Sharing is important later in the process, but the first step calls for individual mapping.

2. The content, skills, and assessments are recorded by month, either by backward or forward mapping (as described in Chapter 2). The monthly format provides a common reference point for all teachers, and it will assist teachers in comparing, analyzing, and integrating the curriculum. Furthermore, applying the monthly format reflects the time-based reality of classroom teaching.

3. When creating the maps, teachers are instructed to use any curricular materials that guide their instruction, including lesson plan books, textbooks, curriculum guides, lessons, and so on. Many teachers find that their daily or weekly plan book is the best source for this information.

4. To record the data, it is crucial that all teachers use a common format. See Figure 3.1 for an example of a mapping template. Using a common format is essential when sharing information between and across grade levels and content areas during the later stages of curriculum mapping. If your district is using curriculum mapping software, the specific format is provided.

5. Recording the content, skills, and assessments for one content area or prep for an academic year requires approximately one half day of release time, or four hours. Language arts at the early elementary level will require additional time. If it takes considerably more time than that, the teachers are probably including too much detail on their maps.

6. Remind teachers that this is a *draft*. Many teachers are perfectionists who want a perfect map. There is no such thing. This first step asks teachers to merely record the data, which is the beginning of the process. Curriculum maps are dynamic, ever-changing, living documents, and they are not intended to be stagnant, finished documents.

7. Give teachers ample time to record content, skills, and assessments on practice maps. This is most effectively completed in a group setting with an experienced curriculum mapping staff developer to prepare teachers for Step 1.

What Is Content?

Content describes the subject matter and can be a topic, theme, specific unit of study, title of a book, or concept. Examples of content include the following:

Math examples
- Addition and subtraction facts
- Estimation

Figure 3.1 Curriculum Mapping Template

Month	Topic/Content	Skills	Assessments

- Place value
- Polynomial functions
- Probability and statistics
- Integers

Language Arts examples
- Paragraph writing
- Personal narrative writing
- *Othello*
- Short stories (including specific titles)
- Poetry (including the specific type)
- Spelling

Social Studies examples
- Manifest destiny
- Progressive era
- Environment
- Citizenship
- Communities
- U.S. Constitution

Science examples
- Photosynthesis
- Cells
- Scientific measurement
- Scientific notation
- Atomic structure
- Plants

Music examples
- Note value
- Time signature
- Baroque-era music
- Composition
- Individual performance

While these are typical content examples, some teachers, as they progress through the initial mapping cycle, find it helpful to break down the content even further. In one district where the adopted math series was organized in a spiraled manner, the teachers chose to organize each month's math content by first identifying the broad conceptual areas as topics and then listing the specific math concepts that were connected to those broad topics as content. The topics and sample conceptual areas are represented in Figure 3.2.

As in math, some teachers find it helpful to organize other content areas by broader topics and subcategorized content. The language arts teachers in one district collaboratively decided to organize their language arts curriculum in the following topics: reading, writing, grammar, and spelling, as illustrated in an excerpt of a fourth grade language arts map presented in Figure 3.3. This type of organization should only occur when teachers come together and arrive at agreed-upon topics.

Figure 3.2   Math Topics and Content

Topic	Content
Mathematical Process	Problem solving Number order
Number Operations and Relationships	Number computing Ordinal numbers Even and odd numbers
Geometry	Shapes Area
Measurement	Time Calendar
Statistics and Probability	Graphing
Fractions and Decimals	Fractional parts
Algebraic Relationships	Patterns

Figure 3.3   Language Arts Topics and Content

Month	Topic	Content
September	Reading	*The Tales of Olga da Polga*
	Writing	Sentences
	Grammar	Subjects and predicates
	Spelling	Short vowel words Double consonant words

By subcategorizing the multifaceted nature of the language arts curriculum, these primary teachers were better able to look at the specific units and lessons taught each month and organize them according to the content topics. This format helped every teacher document where the specific content area and skills were taught, and greatly assisted the curriculum analysis within and across grade levels that occurs later in the curriculum mapping process.

Recording Skills

Skills are the precise expectations or outcomes students are expected to know, and should reflect the content and academic standards. Traditionally, curriculum skills have been documented as behavioral objectives that usually begin with the words "The students will . . ." They are often wordy and, in many cases, do not address the *specific* student expectations. As a result, there is the tendency

Figure 3.4   Action Verbs

Adapt	Differentiate	Model
Adjust	Discuss	Modify
Analyze	Display	Monitor
Apply	Distinguish	Organize
Appraise	Document	Participate
Argue	Draft	Perform
Articulate	Engage	Plan
Ask	Establish	Pose problems
Assess	Estimate	Predict
Brainstorm	Evaluate	Present
Build	Examine	Prioritize
Calculate	Exhibit	Produce
Challenge	Experiment	Propose
Check	Explain	Prove
Classify	Explore	Pursue
Clarify	Express	Question
Collect	Find	Rate
Combine	Gather (evidence, etc.)	Reason
Compare	Generalize	Recognize
Complete	Give (reasons,	Reflect
Compute	examples, etc.)	Represent
Conclude	Help	Research
Conduct	Hypothesize	Respond
Connect	Identify	Retrieve
Consider	Illustrate	Review
Construct	Incorporate	Revise
Contrast	Induce	Role-play
Correct	Inquire	Search
Create	Inspect	Seek
Critique	Instruct	Select
Decide	Integrate	Show
Deduce	Interact	Solve
Defend	Interpret	Structure
Define	Invent	Support
Demonstrate	Investigate	Synthesize
Derive	Judge	Teach
Describe	Justify	Test
Design	Label	Translate
Detect	Locate	Use
Develop	List	Utilize
Devise	Make	Visualize

to describe skills using nebulous terms that are difficult to specifically define, assess, and align to standards. The skills listed on the maps must be precise and reflect active demonstrations of learning. Providing teachers with a list of precise action verbs that include higher-order thinking skills will help broaden their perception of the required skills. See Figure 3.4 for examples of action verbs.

Figure 3.5   Activities Versus Skills

Activity	Rewritten as Skills
Students form a poetry circle	Perform oral poetry reading Demonstrate good eye contact, projection, tone, volume, and articulation
Make a table to solve problems	Solve multiplication problems with products up to 100 Develop a problem-solving table for multiplication problems with products up to 100
Idea map showing photosynthesis	Identify and illustrate the steps of photosynthesis
Create an insect collection	Categorize and label insects by kingdom, phylum, class, order, family genus, and species

Furthermore, for many teachers it is easy to confuse skills with activities, which is apparent in the following examples:

Students

- Form a poetry circle
- Make a table to solve problems
- Idea map showing photosynthesis
- Create a collection of insects

These examples reflect activities that will help students learn the skills but are not, in themselves, skills. However, some of these or other activities may also be reconstructed as performance assessments. Remember, skills must be written concisely, reflect an action, be assessable, and be tied to standards. Figure 3.5 is a list of the activities rewritten in the form of concise skills.

Figure 3.6 presents the fourth grade language arts map excerpt from Figure 3.3 with examples of precise skills.

The Assessment Component

The assessment component requires teachers to document all the ways they assess their students for understanding and mastery of content, skills, and academic standards. Assessments include performance assessments and products. By keeping in mind both formats, teachers are encouraged to go beyond the often more common perception that assessments mean tests and quizzes. When teachers are encouraged to consider all the ways they receive, or could receive, feedback regarding mastery and understanding of precise skills, the assessments become broader, more inclusive, and represent a balance of strategies. It is also

Figure 3.6   Fourth Grade Language Arts Map Sample

Month	Topic and Content	Skills
September	Reading: *The Tales of Olga da Polga*	Read orally with expression Follow along when others are reading aloud Summarize main idea of story Predict outcomes of story
	Writing: Sentences	Identify complete sentences in written examples Recognize run-on sentences in written examples Write complete sentences
	Grammar: Subjects and predicates	Recognize the subject and predicate Identify compound subjects Identify compound predicates Write sentences using single and compound subjects and predicates
	Spelling: Short vowel words Double consonant words	Spell words with short vowels and double consonants Use short vowel words and words with double consonants in sentences

important to note that assessment feedback must include concrete evidence of achievement. While observable performances (speeches, debates, interviews, games, observations, etc.) are critical types of assessments, at particular times during a grading period they must be accompanied with some type of documentation that could include a checklist, scoring guide, or written commentary. When teachers do not document the observations, they often rely on memory or an overall sense of achievement. Recorded assessments of the performance allow teachers to give specific feedback. Criteria on which the performance will be assessed should be shared with students in advance.

Creating balanced assessments complement state-based assessments and encourage students to be more self-directed learners (Costa & Kallick, 2004). Remember, all assessments must be included on the maps: grade level, district and state exams, portfolio checks, preschool and kindergarten screening, and so on. Referring to lists of assessment types can assist teachers as they develop their maps. Figure 3.7 provides such a list.

Including assessments on the maps is a vital component of curriculum development that was formerly missing in most other curriculum processes.

Figure 3.7   Assessment Types

Anecdotal records	Math problems
Book reviews	Observations
Checklists	Oral presentation
Concerts	Performance assessment
Conferences	Poetry
Demonstrations	Posters
Diagrams	Projects
Diorama	Quizzes
Essays	
	• Objective
• Creative	• Short answer
• Personal narrative	
• Expository	Reading response
• Descriptive	Research paper
	Running records
Exhibits	Speeches
Games	Story maps
Graphic organizers	Technical writing papers
In-class discussion	Tests
Interviews	
Journals	• Essay
Lab reports	• Objective
Letters	• Short answer
• Personal	Worksheets
• Business	

Recording, comparing, and analyzing all assessments within and across grade levels and content areas truly encourages the reflection and collaboration that has the potential to increase teacher performance and student achievement. As teachers record their assessment types and strategies, they must take a closer, more analytic view of their assessment practices. This analysis also becomes the basis for creating grade-level or course benchmark assessments, which are covered in more detail in Chapter 4.

Figure 3.8 presents the fourth grade language arts map with assessments.

Standards Alignment and Essential Questions

Aligning the student academic standards to curriculum maps and developing essential questions can be included during the initial mapping process or can occur after the teachers have documented and edited their content, skills, and assessments. (Standards alignment and essential questions are described in detail in Chapter 4.) The timing of this step usually depends upon the teachers' knowledge base and comfort level. Teachers who have a good understanding of the standards, or those who are using a curriculum mapping software program with preloaded standards, may choose to align them as they record the content,

Figure 3.8   Fourth Grade Language Arts Map Excerpt

Month	Topic and Content	Skills	Assessments
September	Reading: *The Tales of Olga da Polga*	Read orally with expression Follow along when others are reading aloud Summarize main idea of story Predict outcomes of story	Observation as students read orally— anecdotal records Class Discussion Reading response journal
	Writing: Sentences	Identify complete sentences Recognize run-on sentences Write complete sentences	Complete sentence game Writing Complete Sentence Worksheet—Homework
	Grammar: Subjects and predicates	Recognize the subject and predicate Identify compound subjects Identify compound predicates Write sentences using compound subjects and predicates	In-class board work—observation Worksheet Completed written sentences
	Spelling: Short vowel words Double consonant words	Spell words with short vowels and double consonants Use short vowel words and words with double consonants in sentences	Spelling game Spelling test Completed sentences

skills, and assessments. Many schools already require that teachers include standards in their weekly lesson plans. Others may feel overwhelmed during this initial step of mapping and will choose to align the standards later in the mapping process. Developing and including essential questions also depends on the teachers' understanding of essential questions. Some may already be using essential questions in their curriculum and will want to include them during Step 1. For others, it is a new concept that will require additional staff development as the mapping process continues. These concepts are addressed in depth in Chapter 4.

Adding Other Components to the Maps

Some teachers inquire about including additional components to the maps, often referring to activities and/or resources. It is not recommended that additional components be included as a requirement at this time, but should be considered during subsequent mapping cycles. As presented in the previous section, many teachers feel overwhelmed as they initially record the content, skills, and assessments, and to be required to add other components can heighten their anxiety. Furthermore, if you are creating maps using a Microsoft Word template adding components beyond content, skills, assessments, essential questions and standards, it can make the maps large and cumbersome and you may want to consider adding resources or specific activities as addendums to the maps. If you choose to purchase a curriculum mapping software program, some incorporate features where additional components are included or can be added.

Coaching During Step 1

In addition to the initial training on the curriculum mapping process, it is helpful to provide coaching sessions for teachers as they record their content, skills, and assessments. These sessions are most beneficial in a one-on-one or small group setting with an experienced curriculum mapping expert. Coaching provides reassurance and support to teachers as they create their initial maps.

The Value of Coaching During Step 1

This mid-sized school district was midway through the process of journal mapping, and many of the high school teachers were having difficulty understanding the difference between content and skills, as well as comprehending the value of the process. The administrators, sensitive to the questions and reservations that were surfacing, asked if I would provide a coaching session at the beginning of their next curriculum mapping workday. Prior to the session, I reviewed a number of their maps, and with permission from specific teachers, I made transparencies of a variety of map excerpts. Together, the high school staff and I viewed the samples on the overhead and jointly edited. By the end of this short session, the teachers could recognize the difference between content and skills and make connections between the content, skills, and assessments. They had a much more clear understanding of curriculum mapping, and they were beginning to see mapping as a dynamic process. As I circulated through the classrooms that afternoon, the comments were much more positive and the maps were more complete. There was an eagerness to complete the maps and proceed to the next step, where they would be viewing other maps in their building and especially those at the middle school. While some reservations and challenges remained, the process became much clearer and the teachers felt more confident.

Concluding Thoughts About Step 1

Step 1 is often the most difficult and time intensive. It is extremely important to provide adequate curriculum mapping training and to allocate the necessary time for teachers to complete their maps. This is the time when administrative support and knowledge about the curriculum mapping process is vital. Administrators must have a good understanding of the process, be invested in the initiative, and provide the appropriate guidance for teachers to be invested in the process as well.

Step 2: Reviewing Groups of Maps

Reviewing the maps is the step in curriculum mapping where teachers review one another's maps independently, not in a group setting. This step often begins at the building level but will eventually take place across buildings. The most meaningful review occurs when teachers read a variety of maps within and across content areas and at various grade levels. However, if your district is initially focusing on a particular content area or groups of courses, the reviewing can occur within those areas.

For most teachers, this is the first time they have been privy to what actually occurs in each other's classrooms, and it is the time when teachers first begin to see the big picture of the curriculum. As teachers review a set of maps, they are instructed to look for the following:

- A clear connection between content, skills, and assessments
- Clear and concise skills. *Are the skills listed as action verbs?*
- A variety of assessments. *Is there a balance of assessments and is there required documentation of observation-type assessments?*
- The possible gaps in content and skills within and across grade levels
- The meaningless redundancies across grade levels and content areas in content and skills. *Are there units or topics that are taught multiple times at multiple grade levels that are redundant (e.g., three years of dinosaur units)?*
- Repetitions in the content and skills. *Does the curriculum reflect a repetition of content and skills that build or spiral?*
- New understandings or the "aha" moments
- Overall questions, comments, or concerns about the curriculum

When planning the editing step, it is important to consider the following:

- Initially teachers will edit the maps within their building.
- Keep the number of maps for each teacher to initially edit to a manageable number. Start with 12–14 maps, as reviewing too many maps especially at the beginning tends to be overwhelming. Teachers will expand the maps they review as subsequent mapping cycles are implemented. The goal is that eventually all teachers will be reviewing all curriculum maps in some fashion as curriculum mapping continues.
- Reviewing 12–14 maps will require approximately three to four hours. Although every teacher will not edit every map, keep in mind that every map will be read and reviewed by a variety of teachers.

- Each group of maps should reflect the horizontal curriculum (within a grade level) and the vertical curriculum (preceding and following a specific grade level). For example, for the first review cycle at the elementary level, teachers could edit maps at their grade level, plus one grade above and one grade below. At the middle school or high school level, teachers will edit all maps within a content area. If the departments are relatively small, they may wish to combine closely connected curriculum areas such as math/science and social studies/English.
- Encourage teachers to take a hard, analytic view of what they're editing. Merely giving the maps a cursory glance will not result in any significant information.
- Continue to emphasize that this is not a time to point fingers or react negatively to what you are reviewing. It is a time to react and respond to what is being edited and to pose questions and concerns in an honest manner in the name of improving the curriculum.
- It is helpful for teachers to have a template to use when recording their findings. See Figure 3.9 for a blank sample form and Figure 3.10 for a completed sample form. This form is a useful tool for teachers to refer to when participating in Step 3, sharing the reviews with colleagues.

Do not rush to the editing step even though teachers will want to edit before all content areas or courses are mapped. If there is not enough information to meaningfully share and analyze, the editing session will be deemed by many as a waste of time. This is often true at the high school level when teachers will want to edit before all courses, or at least the core required courses, within a specific content area are mapped.

Concluding Thoughts About Step 2

Sharing their maps for the initial review is the first time all teachers' individual curriculums have been made public, which, as discussed in Chapter 2, can cause anxiety. Many will not feel comfortable or capable of giving feedback to their colleagues about what they teach. It is crucial that those leading this initiative provide guidance and support and continually reinforce the goal of this process: to create an authentic, consistent, standards-aligned, and student-based curriculum while creating a culture and environment of professionalism and trust.

Step 3: Sharing the Reviews With Colleagues

After all teachers have reviewed a set of maps and recorded their findings on the review form, they come together to share their findings. These structured small-group sessions are designed to allow teachers to openly and honestly present what each has learned as a result of reading through their colleagues' maps. Here are helpful guidelines when organizing this step.

- It is crucial to set the stage for sharing results. Remind teachers that personalities, past performances, or personal beliefs are not part of these sessions. This is the time when teachers merely state what they've discovered as a result of reviewing the maps.

Figure 3.9   Step 2: Reviewing the Maps

This form will help you document the gaps, repetitions, redundancies, and questions you find as you edit the curriculum maps. You will use this form when you meet in small groups to share your edits.

Grade Level	Subject Area	Is there a clear connection between content, skills, and assessments? Are skills described using action verbs?	Gaps: Are there gaps in the content and skills within and across grade levels?	Repetitions or Redundancies: Do repeated skills build and spiral? Are there units of study repeated across multiple grade levels or courses?	Assessment Concerns/ Questions: Are there a variety of assessments? Are they balanced?	Other questions, concerns, and/or new understandings

41

Figure 3.10 Step 2: Reviewing the Maps Sample

This is an example of an excerpt from one teacher's findings from reviewing a group of second, third, and fourth grade math curriculum maps.

Grade Level	Subject Area	Is there a clear connection between content, skills, and assessments? Are skills described using action verbs?	Gaps: Are there gaps in the content and skills within and across grade levels?	Repetitions or Redundancies: Do repeated skills build and spiral? Are there units of study repeated across multiple grade levels or courses?	Assessment Concerns/ Questions: Are there a variety of assessments? Are they balanced?	Other questions, concerns, and/or new understandings
2nd, 3rd, and 4th grades	Math	All maps should be reviewed to use action verbs to describe skills. Estimation and problem solving are listed as separate content in some 3rd grade maps but are listed within the skills in 2nd and 4th—Should this be more consistent? Should they be separated at all grade levels?	Graphing: Some graphing at 2nd grade, no graphing at 3rd grade, and a lot of graphing at 4th grade Estimation: 4th grade lists estimation in the content column but it is not at 2nd and 3rd—How is estimation taught? Could it be a gap? Fractions are not on all 3rd grade maps	What are the specific problem-solving strategies taught at 2nd, 3rd, and 4th grades? It's unclear if it is spiraled. Some geometry skills are repeated in 2nd, 3rd, and 4th grades, but it's unclear what the specific skill expectations are. Are they spiraled or repeated?	Assessments in 2nd grade seem repetitive for each month. More detail would be helpful. Assessments in 3rd and 4th grade are more detailed. How are observations documented?	In 4th grade, what does adding and subtracting large numbers mean? One 4th grade map lists division, geometry, measurement, in the last month. Other 4th grade maps allocate longer amounts of time to these areas earlier in the year. Basic computation skills are taught each year, but how are they taught and assessed to better ensure mastery? Where are literacy skills included in our math curriculum?

- The groups should be composed of 7–8 colleagues from a variety of subject areas and/or grade levels. The small size will give all participants adequate time to share what they have discovered when reviewing curriculum maps. The curriculum mapping coordinators may choose to assign the groups.
- All participants should bring their editing sheets to the meeting. It may be useful to bring hard copies of the maps or have access to computers to access maps if needed.
- It's best that participants follow a protocol for sharing and recording small-group editing results. Assigning participant roles assists the process. Suggested roles include the following:
  - *Recorder:* responsible for recording the issues discussed. See Figure 3.11 for a sample template for recording and Figure 3.12 for an example of a completed template
  - *Timekeeper:* responsible for keeping each person's sharing time to a set number of minutes
  - *Facilitator:* responsible for keeping the conversation on task and continually reminding the group that this is not a time to solve problems, but rather to report what was discovered when editing the maps. It is very easy to stray from presenting findings to attempting to solve the curriculum problems. Addressing the issues will be the focus of the next curriculum mapping steps. If any amount of time is spent discussing problems, the time will quickly elapse.
- The time allotment for this step is 1.5–2 hours.

Concluding Thoughts About Step 3

Up to this point, curriculum mapping has been a time-consuming, labor-intensive endeavor. It's during this step, as teachers come together and present their findings from teacher-generated data, that understanding and relevance of the process begins to surface. These sessions illustrate curriculum strengths and commonalities, but also, and more important, the big picture issues arise that can only surface when cross-content and cross-grade level analysis occurs. This step marks the beginning of new understanding and growth among the entire staff.

Step 4: Reporting the Results of Small Group Work With All Faculty

Following the small-group sessions, the entire faculty at that particular site convenes to present the findings from the small group work. At this time, each recorder reports the group's findings. Those findings are also recorded. The following guidelines will guide this process:

- Again, it is important to set the stage for sharing. Remind everyone that this is not a time to point fingers or make judgments but rather to focus on the curricular areas that need to be addressed.

Figure 3.11 Step 3: Sharing the Reviews With Colleagues

Each small group is composed of 7–8 faculty members representative of a wide range of grade levels.
As you work in small groups and discuss your edited maps, please keep in mind the following:

- Do not try to "solve" anything. This is not the time to judge but to merely state what you found. **KEEP FOCUSED.**
- Record on the form below the gaps, redundancies, meaningful assessments, and new understandings (other) you have discussed.

Recorder: _____ Timekeeper: _____ Facilitator: _____

Other Group Members: _____

Grade Level	Subject Area	Gaps	Redundancies and/or Repetitions Questions/Concerns	Assessment Questions/Concerns	Other Issues

Figure 3.12 Step 3: Sharing the Reviews With Colleagues Sample

This form illustrates sample findings from one group's outcomes from individually reviewing 1st–5th grade math maps.

Each small group is composed of 7–8 faculty members representative of a wide range of grade levels.

As you work in small groups and discuss your edited maps, please keep in mind the following:

- Do not try to "solve" anything. This is not the time to judge but to merely state what you found. **KEEP FOCUSED.**
- Record on the form below the gaps, redundancies, meaningful assessments, and new understandings (other) you have discussed.

Recorder: Bonnie Kreger   Timekeeper: Claudia Kay   Facilitator: Jeff Adler

Other Group Members: Fred Lenstra, Mae Wand, Mary Kaiser, Brian Hanrah, Katie Clark

Grade Level	Subject Area	Gaps	Redundancies and/or Repetitions Questions/Concerns	Assessment Questions/Concerns	Other Issues
1st–5th grades	Math	Graphing: Some graphing at 1st and 2nd grade, no graphing at 3rd grade, a strong emphasis on graphing at 4th grade, and no graphing at 5th grade Estimation: 4th grade lists estimation in the content column but it is not at 2nd and 3rd and 5th. How is estimation taught? Could it be a gap? Problem Solving is separate content at 3rd grade but not at 2nd and 4th. Is it a gap in 2nd and 4th? Fractions: Possible gaps. Inconsistent within and between grade levels. Not all 3rd grades teach fractions, 4th grade emphasizes different skills, and 5th grade has heavy emphasis. Statistics and Probability: Some taught at 2nd, none at 3rd or 4th, and a strong emphasis in 5th	Some geometry skills are repeated in 2nd, 3rd, 4th, and 5th grades but it's unclear what the specific skill expectations are. Are they spiraled or repeated? How does place value content and skills in 5th grace connect to place value skills in 3rd and 4th grades? Is it spiraled?	Most assessments in 1st grade are observation. Are checklists or rubrics used? What other types of assessments are administered at 1st grade? Assessments in 2nd grade seem repetitive for each month. More detail is needed. Assessments in some 3rd and 4th grade are more detailed. Some provide good examples. Good balance of assessments in 5th grade. When rubrics are listed, can we all access them? Is chapter test enough assessment information?	Review all maps for using action verbs to describe skills. Explore the amount of time teachers at each grade level allocate to specific math topics. The time allotment within and across grade levels varies. 5th grade integrates some literacy skills in their math curriculum. Should we all be looking at literacy integration? Basic computation skills are taught 1st–5th grades, but how are they taught and assessed to better ensure mastery?

45

- Each recorder reports the findings from his or her particular small group.
- The findings are categorized by grade level or content area and recorded on flip charts or digital projector for all to see.
- It is highly recommended that an external facilitator, consultant, or teacher leader facilitate the session and record the findings.
- The building principal must be in attendance.
- This session will take approximately 2 hours.

Concluding Thoughts About Step 4

When teachers reach this step, profound changes occur. Faculty members begin to see their district's true curriculum, its positive aspects, and the areas that need further work. Curriculum change and direction are based on teacher data, *not* the top-down interests or concerns of administration. The following two stories describe this evolution.

A curriculum leader that had participated in a *Curriculum Mapping Trainer of Trainers* two-day workshop that I had facilitated the previous spring sent the first story to me. Her story describes her experience with a very reluctant teacher.

The Resistant Mapper

The first day I had a REALLY negative teacher; she is a great sixth grade instructor, but she was certain that curriculum mapping was a waste of her time, and she was not quiet about it! She complained about each step. The next session she came in and said, "I want you to know that I called my friend in Wyoming to complain; they are doing the mapping there. I expected her to agree with me, but she said, 'Shut up, quit complaining and do the map. You'll love it when you're done. It's a great process.' That isn't what I wanted to hear, but I came with an open attitude today." Later that morning, when I checked on her in her room, she said, "This is great! I love it! I'm going to enlarge the map, laminate it, and post it in my classroom so the students can see where we have been and where we are going." I was shocked!

After the individual editing, the small group review, and the large group discussion, she said, "This is the best thing we have ever done for professional development! We need to do language arts." When I explained that the leadership team had chosen language arts for the second year, she said, "We can't wait. This is too important. Can't we skip all that other workshop nonsense and get started with language arts?"

Several others agreed that they wanted to get going on language arts too! What a turnaround! I told that teacher I was going to make her the poster child for mapping; she said she'd speak to any reluctant teacher. She's sold.

The next story describes one district's change of heart as they completed the first cycle of curriculum mapping.

One District's Evolution

This was one of the first districts in which I facilitated the mapping process for an entire school year. The district had made a commitment that curriculum mapping would be the primary focus for curriculum work and staff development. We had taken significant time to meet with teacher leaders to plan the curriculum mapping process, making sure that sufficient time and staff training were in place before we began the process. From all preliminary indications, there was support from the initial committee for the process.

In the fall, I worked with all the staff for a full day to introduce mapping and to provide support and coaching as they created their maps. Additional staff development hours were allocated throughout the fall and early winter months for the teachers to complete Step 1. I returned to the district when the teachers had completed Step 1 to provide editing directions and be available for questions. Each time I worked with the staff, it was apparent that many were not happy to be mapping the curriculum. It's never a good sign when the consultant arrives at a school and no one will make eye contact. I definitely got the feeling that they wanted the "mapping lady" to pack up her mapping ideas and go home!

I returned in early spring for the small group and large group review, which happened to be scheduled on the last day before spring break. When I arrived, there was again no eye contact and definitely no welcome greeting. Shortly after they congregated in the cafeteria and were assigned to their small groups, I could sense the atmosphere changing. This resistant staff began to share their curriculum findings. The conversations were rich, focused, and productive. The evolution had begun.

As they transitioned to the large-group sharing session, the atmosphere was totally different. When they began to share their findings, the professionalism and positive attitude in the room was palpable. As each group reported their findings, there were nods of agreement and anecdotal supportive comments throughout the room. As the large-group sharing session came to an end, there was eagerness and urgency among the staff to continue to work together to address the issues. Specific plans were made to create an action plan before the end of school for summer work in preparation for the next school year.

This episode confirmed my belief in the tremendous power of curriculum mapping. I will never forget that as I left that afternoon, a number of teachers actually looked at me and offered their best wishes for a good spring break!

This episode marked a pivotal point in my own learning. Just as the staff experienced an "evolution," so did I as I witnessed the strength of this collaborative, reflective process. It was just the beginning.

Step 5: Developing an Action Plan

The final step of the initial curriculum mapping cycle is to create a plan of action based on the large-group findings. Grade level leaders, department chairs, specific classroom teachers, the curriculum director, building administrator, or curriculum mapping coordinator can facilitate the planning process.

The following steps provide guidelines and suggestions for going forward and addressing the issues.

- Categorize the issues by
  - Grade level and/or content area
  - Combination of grade levels or content areas
  - Building
  - District

- Decide on a definite timetable, including an estimated time frame for addressing each specific issue. Some obvious issues can be addressed in a relatively short time frame, while other issues will require long-term, districtwide involvement.
- Establish a committee or responsible parties to address the specific issues.
- As the plan is implemented and each specific issue is resolved, the responsible parties, or committee members, will report back to the faculty and the appropriate changes will be made on the maps. See Figure 3.13 for a planning guide template and Figure 3.14 for an example of a completed action plan.

During some large-group sharing sessions, particular issues can be resolved immediately. The following story illustrates this point.

"You Mean I Don't Have to Teach Dinosaurs?"

A large-group review session revealed that only one of the four fourth grade teachers was teaching a dinosaur unit. It was also noted that all second grade teachers included dinosaur units in the second grade curriculum. As this was recorded on the flip chart as a possible gap, one fourth grade teacher jumped to her feet and asked, "I'm the one teaching dinosaurs, and I'm wondering why I'm the only one?" The other fourth grade teachers responded that they had decided two years ago that it would remain in second grade. She looked surprised and relieved as she said, "No one told me, but I am SO happy because I hated teaching that unit!" Everyone laughed but at the same time realized how little communication had been taking place within or across grade levels.

It made one wonder how long this would have continued had there not been mapping. It also raises a question about the mind-set of her students as they once again were taught the dinosaur unit.

Figure 3.13 Action Plan Form

Curricular Issue	Grade Level and/or Content Area	Responsible person to oversee the process of addressing the issue	Committee Members: Those who will serve on the committee to address the issue	Plan: What will need to happen to resolve this issue?	Timeline: The estimated amount of time required to address the issue	Date to Be Completed

Figure 3.14 Action Plan Sample

Curricular Issue	Grade Level and/or Content Area	Responsible person to oversee the process of addressing the issue	Committee Members: Those who will serve on the committee to address the issue	Plan: What will need to happen to resolve this issue?	Timeline: The estimated amount to time required to address the issue	Date to Be Completed
Integrating literacy skills with math curriculum	1st–5th grade language arts and math courses	Brian Hanrah and Katie Clark	Representatives from all elementary grades (1st–5th): Brian Hanrah, Katie Clark, Fred Lenstra, Mae Wand, Mary Kaiser, Jeff Adler, Claudia Kay	Schedule meeting time to organize the following: Research professional resources (e.g., journal articles, speakers, texts) for strategies regarding math and language arts integration Collect and record key math vocabulary for each grade to be included in the curriculum Examine the 5th grade curriculum where they are integrating some language skills Develop specific literacy integration guidelines and strategies for each grade level based on the committee's research	6 weeks	Report with recommendations will be presented at the staff meeting on February 15

Concluding Thoughts About Step 5

While this step is clearly the beginning of the evolution, it can also be the time that curriculum mapping can lose momentum. Many times I have heard comments such as, "Finally, we've completed our maps, talked about them, and now we're finished with that project!" I have also had administrators proudly show me their completed binder of maps. This is clearly not the desired outcome of mapping and is reminiscent of the traditional curriculum that consists of completed, stagnant curriculum documents stored in binders. It certainly does not reflect the dynamic and living curriculum that is the intended outcome of the mapping process. To continue the evolutionary work begun in the first mapping cycle, a concerted effort from all stakeholders and organized planning must be in place to continue the momentum. Strategies for implementing the action plan and ways to use the maps as dynamic and meaningful tools to improve student achievement are outlined in the next section and addressed at length in Chapter 4.

Step 6: Implementing the Action Plan and Beyond

Continuing the cycle of curriculum mapping will include a variety of steps based on what has been accomplished and presented during the first cycle. The primary task will be to map the remaining content areas and/or courses. As these maps are completed, teachers will again complete the steps described above.

Other issues may include the following and will be addressed in Chapter 4:

- Create follow-up and accountability measures for the strategies outlined in the action plan as a result of the first mapping cycle
- Align curriculum and academic standards
- Develop essential questions
- Look for opportunities for integration of curriculum and clustering of related topics, themes, priorities, and academic standards across content and related arts areas
- Add resources and/or activities, if desired
- Establish a curriculum mapping communication process
- Establish priorities for continued curriculum work and staff development based on mapping data and other external issues

Implementing the Action Plan and Beyond

[Strength] can come when power is given through support and opportunity for responsible decision-making and capacity building.

—Pearl G. Solomon (2003, p. 46)

As the first cycle of curriculum mapping concludes, it is easy to fall back on the historic notion that the curriculum is now finished, and the initiative can lose momentum. Unless there is sound understanding of the long-term benefits of curriculum mapping, and a well-articulated plan, there is a very high risk that curriculum mapping will not survive beyond the initial cycle.

The next sections present suggestions for creating a long-term plan that addresses the next steps beyond the first cycle of mapping, describe possible communication structures, and illustrate the powerful ways mapping can determine the direction for staff development opportunities and continued curriculum improvement.

THE LONG-TERM PLAN

Movement beyond the first cycle of mapping will not follow a linear path. Some tasks will be required for all teachers, and others will pertain to specific groups of teachers. Figure 4.1 illustrates the possible directions mapping can take. Each component of the graphic is described in the following sections.

Figure 4.1 Steps for Continuing Curriculum Mapping Beyond the Initial Cycle

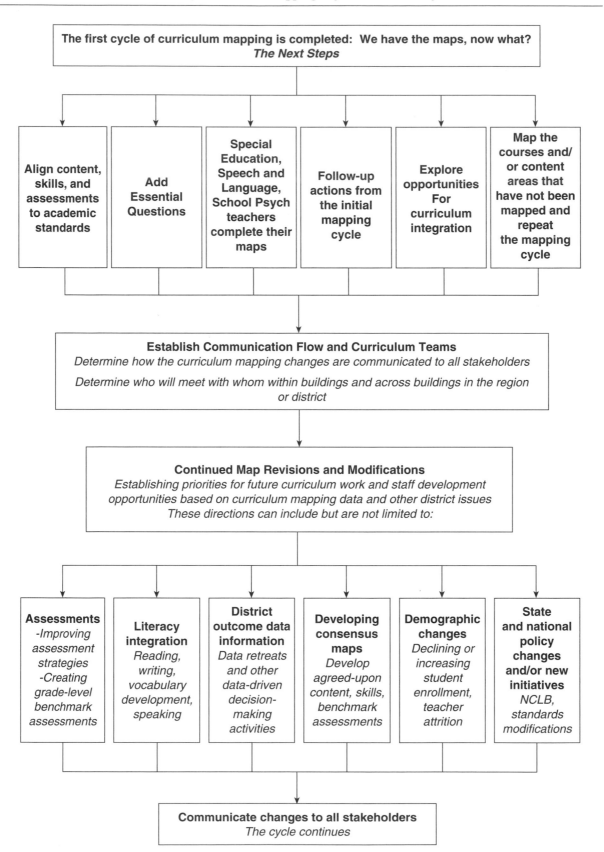

STANDARDS ALIGNMENT

As discussed in Chapter 1, aligning academic standards and curriculum is a vital issue facing most school districts. Curriculum map information provides the authentic curriculum data to meaningfully align with academic standards.

When aligning the content, skills, and assessment to your state's academic standards, two issues must be considered. First, teachers must have a clear understanding of what alignment consists of. It is not what is called "coverage," which was addressed in Chapter 3. True alignment is teaching content and skills that are intricately linked to standards with the appropriate assessments to provide evidence of standards feedback. Teachers should have a working knowledge of the standards.

Second, a consistent method of documenting the standards on the maps must be established. Teachers can either record the specific standards and benchmarks on the maps using the code or numbering system, or they may choose to record the entire standard and/or benchmark. Merely using the number or codes does not offer the language of the specific standard, and requires teachers to have the official standards document for referral. However, typing all of the standards language is time intensive. Some districts find a combination of both strategies: using the codes and an abbreviated description of the standard. If your district is using a curriculum mapping software program, the standards will be downloaded in the software, allowing a much more efficient method of documenting the standards.

As teachers cross-reference the standards with skills and assessments, they are able to identify what standards are being taught and assessed, the length of time spent on each standard, how often the standard is repeated, and which standards are not being taught and assessed. When teachers identify a standard not being taught and assessed, they should address the following questions:

- Is the standard measured on the state exams?
- Is the standard important for us to be teaching, based on our professional knowledge about what students should know and be able to do?
- If the standard is not on the state exam, and as professionals we don't believe it is of vital importance, how much time, if any, should be spent teaching that particular standard?

When teachers collaboratively analyze the standards and prioritize them according to the above criteria, they can identify those standards that carry the most weight, often referred to as the "power standards."

ESSENTIAL QUESTIONS

Essential questions provide a focus for the lesson or unit of study and help reveal the complexities and richness of a subject (Wiggins & McTighe, 1998). They pull together skills and encourage teachers and students to go much deeper into the content. Continually posing these guided questions provides opportunities for students to think out of the box and encourages their natural curiosity to surface. This type of inquiry helps students to think about how they personally relate to the topic. As teachers develop essential questions, the following inquiries can help to guide their thinking about the unit or topic:

- Why is this unit or topic of value to my students?
- What are the most important elements to teach about this topic, given the allotted amount of time?
- How can I best share these key elements with my students to assist their understanding?

When mapping the curriculum, there isn't a best time to introduce the concept of essential questions. Some teachers are more comfortable developing essential questions at the beginning of the mapping process. For them, it makes sense to use the essential questions when conceptualizing the big picture of the unit of study. For others, essential questions are easier to develop once the content, skills, and assessments are clear. Some may already use essential questions and will include them as they proceed through Step 1 of mapping. For those reasons, it often works best to choose a time midway through the mapping process to introduce essential questions. A separate workshop on essential questions should be offered by a staff developer well trained in the subject, and ample time should be allowed for teachers to develop their own essential questions. Figure 4.2 illustrates examples of essential questions.

SPECIAL EDUCATION AND OTHER SUPPORT STAFF TEACHERS

As addressed in Chapter 3, this is the time when the special education and other support staff can view the general education maps and begin to create their own maps. General and special education teachers should meet and discuss the modified format of the special education maps. Understanding that the special education teachers' maps are based on the general education maps, a consistent format should be established among special education teachers.

Speech and language teachers and school psychologists will want to view special and general education maps and then develop their own maps accordingly. The structure of their maps can also reflect an agreed-upon modified format.

FOLLOW-UP FROM THE FIRST MAPPING CYCLE

The issues from the first curriculum mapping cycle need to be addressed. Those issues will involve the staff members directly connected to the specific issue. As covered in Chapter 3, some issues will be relatively easy to address, while others will require long-term attention. When these issues are resolved and communicated to the staff, the revisions are made on the maps and the committees working on these issues are dismantled.

Figure 4.2   Essential Questions Sample

Course: Family and Consumer Education Unit: Parenting Time: 5 weeks Grade Level: Grades 11–12 • What is a good parent? • Can anyone be adequately prepared to be a parent? • What should you know about children before becoming a parent?
Unit: Winter Time: 4 weeks Grade Level: Kindergarten • How is winter different from other seasons? • How does winter affect people and animals? • Does everyone experience winter the same way?
Course: Shakespeare Unit: Othello Time: 3 weeks Grade Level: 11 • Why read Shakespeare? • How can the themes of *Othello* be applied to present-day society? • What are the similarities and differences of the goals of language from Shakespeare's time to the present day?
Course: Language Arts Unit: Newspaper Time: 6 weeks Grade Level: 8 • Why do people read the newspaper? • How do readers influence what gets printed in newspapers? • How do newspapers influence society? • Is the newspaper a good source for news?

The results of these modifications may also uncover other problems and concerns that need attention. These issues also need to be communicated to the staff and a plan established for addressing the identified concerns.

Opportunities for Curriculum Integration

The first cycle of curriculum mapping provides a monthly record of what and when specific content and skills are taught that assist all teachers to identify common skills, interconnections, relationships, and priorities among skills and standards. As teachers examine the maps, they can develop strategies and plans for curriculum integration. For example a relatively easy method to begin integrating the curriculum is by altering the sequencing of topics so similar units can coincide (i.e., studying the Holocaust in history while reading *The Diary of Anne Frank* in English). As the mapping cycles continue, the potential for integration will increase and evolve into meaningful learning experiences for students.

MAPPING COURSES/CONTENT AREAS NOT PREVIOUSLY MAPPED

As described in earlier chapters, initially districts may decide not to map all courses and content areas. At the completion of the first curriculum mapping cycle, those courses and content areas need to be mapped. As those maps are completed, the cycle of data collection, editing, and small and large group review is repeated.

Exploring Student Feeder Patterns and Subsequent Communication Flow Patterns

Curriculum maps become the resource for sharing information and resolving curricular issues. However, to facilitate good communication about the maps, an effective and efficient communication system must be in place. Heidi Hayes Jacobs developed a model for communicating curriculum among grade levels and buildings in a district. The following sections describe a similar communication model, including protocols to facilitate the communication process.

When establishing a communication system, it is important to first look at the way students progress through the school district. Figure 4.3 illustrates the communication flow pattern of a district that consists of five kindergarten–Grade Five buildings, two separate middle schools, and one high school.

As illustrated in Figure 4.3, elementary school children can flow within or across the elementary school buildings within the district or region. Specific elementary school children travel into a specific middle school. Washington, Lincoln, and Kennedy School children proceed to Blackhawk Middle School, and children attending Roosevelt and Jefferson Schools progress to Cherokee Middle School. All students from both Blackhawk and Cherokee Middle Schools flow directly to Martin Luther King High School.

The communication system should mimic the students' travel patterns and flow back and forth between the buildings. This, again, requires teachers to look beyond their classrooms and separate buildings to the regional or districtwide system.

Curriculum Teams: A Structure for Sharing Information

Once the teachers in each building have progressed through the first cycle of mapping and the maps are in good working order, it is time for them to share their curriculum maps across buildings. This can occur in a variety of ways,

Figure 4.3   Big Picture: Communication Flow Sample

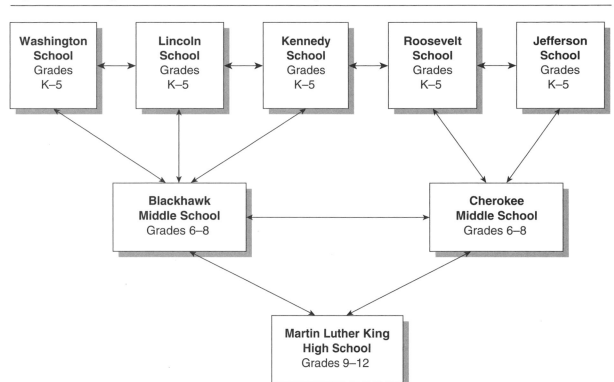

but should closely follow the mapping cycle of reading, editing, and discussing the maps in small and large groups.

When teachers begin to look at the maps across buildings, it is not necessary for all teachers to meet. Representatives from each site can meet and speak for their colleagues, as the curriculum map information is current and with the aid of technology can be easily accessed and shared. The communication systems in each building and across buildings can be facilitated and organized in the form of a curriculum advisory team or, as Jacobs refers to them, curriculum councils and cabinets (Jacobs, 1997, 2001). The terms *teams, boards, councils,* and *cabinets* are used interchangeably in this book.

The curriculum advisory teams are established at each building site with representation from each grade level, each content area, special education, support services, and related arts, including the building administrator and media specialist. Meeting at or around each grading period is suggested. The educators serving on the team gather curriculum information from their colleagues at staff, department, or grade-level meetings and/or from individual teachers. As issues arise, they are presented to the curriculum team for review and discussion, and plans are established for resolution. There are larger grade-level-specific curriculum teams that would each represent all elementary school, all middle school, and all high school buildings within a district. Representatives from those curriculum teams feed into the overarching, districtwide or region boards. Figure 4.4 illustrates a model of how curriculum councils can be structured within each building and across the district, using the district information from Figure 4.3.

Figure 4.4   Configuration of Curriculum Teams and Communication Patterns

K–5 Building Site-Based Curriculum Team	K–5 Building Site-Based Curriculum Team	K–5 Building Site-Based Curriculum Team	K–5 Building Site-Based Curriculum Team	K–5 Building Site-Based Curriculum Team
Representatives from all areas: grade levels, related arts, media, special education, speech & language, etc. **Meets at or around each grading period**	Representatives from all areas: grade levels, related arts, media, special education, speech & language, etc. **Meets at or around each grading period**	Representatives from all areas: grade levels, related arts, media, special education, speech & language, etc. **Meets at or around each grading period**	Representatives from all areas: grade levels, related arts, media, special education, speech & language, etc. **Meets at or around each grading period**	Representatives from all areas: grade levels, related arts, media, special education, speech & language, etc. **Meets at or around each grading period**

Districtwide Elementary Curriculum Team
Representation from all Elementary Buildings
Meets three times per year determined by the council members

Middle School Curriculum Team	Middle School Curriculum Team
Representatives from all areas: grade levels, related arts, media, special education, speech & language, etc. **Meets at or around each grading period**	Representatives from all areas: grade levels, related arts, media, special education, speech & language, etc. **Meets at or around each grading period**

Districtwide Middle School Curriculum Team
Representation from both middle school buildings.
Meets three times per year determined by the council members

District Curriculum Team
Representation from Elementary Curriculum Council, Middle School Curriculum Council, and High School Curriculum Council
Meets three times per year usually following the elementary, middle, and high school council meetings

High School Curriculum Team
Representation from all areas:
grade levels,
content areas,
related arts, media,
special education,
speech & language, etc.
Meets at or around each grading period

CURRICULUM TEAM STRUCTURE

To ensure the success of the curriculum team, it is important that they be well organized and follow a definite protocol. The following are curriculum board protocol suggestions:

- Consider having teachers rotate their membership after serving a predetermined length of time.
- Establish a definite meeting time and schedule.
- The chairperson of the team should prepare an agenda and post it for all faculty.
    - The agenda will be based on the feedback and suggestions from the building councils and/or state and national information and policy changes that will impact curriculum.
    - A chairperson can be designated at the first meeting.

- The meetings are open to anyone who would like to attend.
- Consider possible compensation in time, money, or benefits for those serving on the teams.
- Prepare a roles and responsibilities description of the curriculum team members.
- Administrators should be in attendance.
- A school board member may be included.

GATHERING INFORMATION
FOR THE CURRICULUM TEAM

As curriculum mapping evolves, teachers who have not traditionally met on a regular basis will begin to meet in various settings to identify curriculum issues. These issues can arise anytime as teachers and administrators meet during grade-level meetings, cross-grade-level meetings, department meetings, cross-department meetings, all-faculty meetings, administrative meetings, and/or informal conversations. As part of the communication system, when issues arise, it is important that teachers have a protocol in place for documenting the issues to be shared with the curriculum team representatives. Figure 4.5 presents a form that should be completed and turned in to the curriculum team representative. The issue can then be added to the agenda for the next curriculum team meeting.

As one school administrator shared:

Without clear documentation of what goes on when the teachers in my district meet, we don't have any idea what the issues are. We don't need another committee without a clear purpose that reflects the teachers concerns. (Curriculum director, personal communication, August 2004)

Curriculum Meeting Protocol				
Date:				
The following teachers met:	**Grade Level**	**Content Area**	**Building(s)**	**Administrator**

Purpose or context of meeting:

Recommendation for curriculum revision:

Based on the following evidence:

Follow-up plans:

Possible meeting topics and/or issues could include the following:

- A new course offering (e.g., integrated history and English course)
- Cross-content area skill requirements (e.g., particular math skills required in science courses)
- A unit of study change reflective of a particular teacher and/or student interest (e.g., a focus on Australia as a result of travel to Australia, or the addition of a new student from another country)
- Classroom student assessment results indicating the need for pacing modifications in curriculum and instruction
- New data from standardized test results illustrating the need for modification in schedule, skill emphasis, or assessments in a particular grade level, content area, or building

CONTINUED REVISION, MODIFICATION, AND GROWTH

Establishing Priorities for Future Curriculum Work and Staff Development

At this point, all teachers have created their maps and entered them on the computer. The obvious gaps and repetitions have been resolved, the curriculum maps are aligned to standards, assessments have been clearly documented, and essential questions have been developed. The maps have become dynamic, living documents and the most valuable source of district curriculum information. A communication system is in place that facilitates curriculum data-driven conversation and meaningful curriculum change. However, the potential value of the curriculum maps has just begun to be realized. As the curriculum is continually reviewed and internal and external circumstances are considered, directions for curriculum work and staff development evolve.

As research suggests, teachers and administrators are turning away from one-shot inservice days to well-planned models of ongoing collaboration and reflection based on the specific needs of the district (Rasmussen, Hopkins, & Fitzpatrick, 2004). These staff development opportunities must be based on events and occurrences deeply embedded in the day-to-day realities of classroom practice (Guskey, 2000). The analysis of reality-based curriculum maps creates the focus for teachers and administrators to set clear, data-generated, student-centered staff development goals and direction. This collaboration removes barriers between teachers and administrators as they publicly analyze the current curriculum map data and make choices according to the district needs.

The following sections offer specific curriculum work and staff development examples based on the curriculum mapping outcomes. These directions are the result of digging deeper into the curriculum mapping data and, in some cases, are influenced by other state and national policies.

Assessment Issues

Based on curriculum map analysis, narrow and repetitive assessments are often curriculum concerns shared by many teachers. Creating a balanced assessment system is the goal and many times guides the direction for assessment staff development. This was the case with the following school district.

I Don't Know How to Do It Any Differently

In a small rural K–12 school, the teachers had just completed the first cycle of mapping. The repetitive and narrow assessment methods were issues that concerned many of the teachers. A veteran high school social studies teacher stood up in front of the staff and said, "I am an example of the teacher who repetitively listed test, quiz, homework, test, quiz, homework as my assessments because that IS how I assess. I know that probably isn't the best way to assess all of my students, but I don't know how to do it any different. That was how I was assessed as a student, and I really didn't learn any other methods in college or during my teaching career. If I'm going to change my way of assessing kids, I'm going to need some help." As the conversation continued, it was apparent there were other teachers who shared his concern. Learning more about alternative assessment strategies and how to best implement them became a focus for staff development and was included in their district's staff development plan. I am convinced that this conversation would never have taken place and been acted upon had it not been for curriculum mapping.

Expanding assessment strategies can also extend to developing common grade level or course benchmark assessments based on agreed-upon skills at each grade level. This assessment strategy is an important component of developing consensus maps that will be addressed later in this chapter.

Literacy Integration

As described in Chapter 1, strong cross-curricular literacy instruction is vital for student success and achievement and is a strong component of No Child Left Behind legislation. As the curriculum maps are continually reviewed and modified, adding literacy skills across the curriculum is an essential goal. To adequately address the literacy integration issues, it is necessary to provide teachers with information about the types of literacy skills needed to enhance instruction. Many non-language-arts teachers don't realize the wide array of literacy skills that can and should be included across the curriculum. Because it is impossible for every teacher to teach every literacy skill, teachers should decide who is teaching the skill, whether the particular skill should be taught across the curriculum, and how much time can reasonably be allocated for the specific skill instruction. Non-language-arts teachers may believe that these particular literacy skills take up valuable content-specific instructional time.

However, in the long term, their students will have the tools to enable them to better comprehend the content.

The following examples illustrate literacy guidelines that reflect reading, writing, speaking, and listening skills across all curricular areas.

Text Structures and Features

According to Jacque Karbon (2004), Reading Consultant for the Wisconsin Department of Public Instruction, assisting students to understand text structures and text features are key to improved reading comprehension across all curricular areas. When students understand the way content-specific texts are organized and structured, they are better able to organize what they are reading and in turn better able to comprehend what they are reading. For example, illustrating to students that science texts are organized in a cause-and-effect manner, while social studies texts are often organized in chronological order based on a timeline, provides valuable prereading information.

Assisting students to recognize the relevance of captions, subtitles, marginal notes, parenthetical definitions, headings, footnotes, bold print and italicized words, graphics, tables, charts, graphs, review questions, and parts of the textbook, as well as how these features work together to create meaning in the text, can also enhance understanding (Forget, 2004). Students often do not understand the value of these features and skip over this information. Allocating instructional time to point out these features and the ways they enhance text understanding greatly assists student learning and comprehension. In addition, these skills will strengthen students' performance on standardized exams.

These types of strategies can be integrated across all curricular areas and documented on the curriculum maps.

Writing Across the Curriculum

Writing skills that include grammar, editing, and revising are also literacy components that need to be addressed consistently by all teachers. The types of writing, especially the addition of technical writing skills, can be incorporated in nonlanguage arts classes.

Speaking and Listening Skills

Many teachers require students to present papers, debates, and projects in relation to the particular content area. Judging their performances not only for the content information but also incorporating an assessment component that judges their speaking ability emphasizes the relevance of oral presentation skills. Using common scoring rubrics for speaking and listening across all curricular areas creates a consistent framework for assessment and integration. These scoring guides become part of the assessments included on the curriculum maps.

The following two stories illustrate how two different high school departments began to look at the literacy components of their curriculum as they examined their maps for literacy integration.

A group of high school social studies and science teachers were examining their maps for literacy integration and discussing the writing element. As I approached them, I asked if they incorporated any type of writing within their classes, and if they did, how did they assess the punctuation and mechanics elements. They responded that they required some writing and their district used the six-trait writing scoring guide, but they admitted they didn't feel comfortable using it. As the conversation continued, it was apparent that if these teachers were to make a conscious effort to effectively assess student writing within their content area, additional staff development was necessary for all staff to learn how to effectively use the six-trait writing scoring guide within all content areas. As a result of mapping, this issue became a staff development goal.

Examining content-specific vocabulary is also an area of integrating literacy skills across the curriculum. Some teachers elect to include a separate component within the content and skills section of the maps that explicitly lists the content-specific vocabulary for the particular unit of study.

Math vocabulary specific to geometry was a topic that surfaced among a group of math teachers as they examined their maps. The following section describes their discussion.

When the high school math department examined their curriculum maps, they noted that one of the teachers listed the specific vocabulary words for each unit of study in the skills section of his map. The other math teachers, who represented the more veteran teachers in the math department, had not listed the vocabulary on their maps. Although they believed it was important, it was just not an area they explicitly focused on. As a result of their conversation and the focus on literacy integration, they decided, as a department, that the specific vocabulary for each math unit would be listed as a separate content area with specific vocabulary skills and appropriate assessments.

DATA RETREAT RESULTS AND CURRICULUM MAPPING

Data retreats and/or other data analysis activities assist teachers and administrators to determine the achievement trends of students and overall patterns of program quality. These events generate vital information that directly impacts curriculum mapping, requiring both processes to work in tandem. The following section, offered by Allison Crean, a data analysis staff developer at InformEd (www.informededucators.com), describes how these processes create increased communication, analysis, and action for all stakeholders.

When a school team analyzes its data, the focus is often on outcome and demographic information. Findings from a school's outcome data reflect the degree to which students demonstrate particular knowledge and/or skills as well as the degree to which the school or district has achieved specified goals. Demographic data describes particular student characteristics that further pinpoints issues within a school and allows for more specific strategies for change.

At some point, the dialogue surrounding these analyses must go beyond static outcomes and student characteristics and turn to the dynamics of how the school goes about its business. Schools cannot directly change student results nor the characteristics of the student populations they serve. What is directly under a school's control are the processes under which it works. Curriculum is a major source of process data, as it reflects how educators within the school are aligning their work to the state or district's learning standards, delivering instruction, and measuring their impact.

Curriculum mapping provides rich data that details the instructional process from teacher to teacher, grade to grade, throughout the region or school district. When gaps, redundancies, or general weaknesses in the curriculum are discovered, school teams should cross-reference student outcomes to see if and how those curricular limitations are having an impact on student performance. Similarly, if a school finds within its outcome data that students are performing weakly on particular skills within a subject area, they should cross-reference curriculum maps to see if and how that skill is being taught, and whether there are opportunities to strengthen the curriculum to facilitate enhanced student learning and hence, better student outcomes going forward.

Understanding specific outcomes, particularly related to student learning, is a critical piece of school improvement. Yet schools must also have access to process data, especially curriculum data, which allow educators to move from discussing "what" the outcomes say to "how" we can improve. Pulling these data sources together is imperative to help schools prioritize the actions they will take and make well-informed decisions related to student instruction.

Developing Consensus Maps

Consensus maps are maps that reflect teacher agreed-upon core content, essential skills, and benchmark assessments. These are often the maps that illustrate what teachers are responsible for teaching in a given school year and are appropriate to share with the public. Although they are based on the teacher's individual maps, they are much less detailed.

To develop these maps, teachers must come to consensus by analyzing the current maps and identifying the core content, essential skills, and benchmark assessments that all students in a particular grade level or course should know (Nicholas, 2004). This analysis requires

- examining current maps and then comparing them within and across grade levels or particular courses. This can occur independently, and then in small and large group settings;
- an understanding of the power standards—where they appear on the curriculum maps and how they align to skills. These become the essential skills that guide consensus building;
- an investigation of current assessment methods and the development of grade-level or course benchmark assessments that can better assess the core skills and can prepare students for the specific skills assessed on high stakes exams. The benchmark assessments can include the types of vocabulary, the structure of the test questions, and types of writing included on the state exams;
- an exploration of the sequence of particular skills in relation to learning outcomes, required cross-curricular skills, and the schedule of the state exams.

Consensus maps can also include specific book choices at each grade level or course, field trip experiences, and/or specific modified curriculums for particular groupings of students.

Demographic Changes

In many districts, declining or increasing student enrollment and teacher attrition also contribute to curriculum modifications. Enrollment changes very often dictate the addition, elimination, or combination of courses. Furthermore, as teachers leave the district, their maps provide the content, skills, and assessment foundation for the creation of the new maps reflective of the new teacher.

State and National Policy Changes and/or New Initiatives

External changes can occur that will influence the curriculum and require modifications on the maps. These changes could include modifications in state standards, changes in the statewide testing schedule, and/or federal mandates such as the current No Child Left Behind legislation.

Using Technology

As noted throughout this book, using technology is the efficiency vehicle that facilitates the ever-changing dynamics of curriculum mapping. To make the ongoing revisions and modifications and to share the results within and across grade levels, buildings and regions, technology is imperative.

For many districts, implementing a specific curriculum mapping software program takes mapping beyond merely recording the data on a Microsoft Word template to searching and analyzing data, and generating useful curriculum reports for all stakeholders. Chapter 5 presents criteria for choosing a software program and descriptions of various curriculum software programs.

5

Curriculum
Mapping Software

People in school today can expect a lifetime in which knowledge itself will radically change—not only in its details but its structures; so that the mark of a truly educated man will no longer be how much or even how variously he knows, but how quickly and how completely he can continually learn.

—Richard Kostelanetz (1986, p. 77)

Since the inception of curriculum mapping in the early 1980s, technology has made an enormous impact on the potential uses of data. Initially, curriculum maps were handwritten, and then, in most cases, teachers entered their maps into the computer using a word processing program. The computer maps enabled teachers to efficiently revise and modify their individual maps. Soon, many districts began to enter the maps into their districtwide network, which greatly enhanced the capability for teachers to share their maps within and across grade levels and buildings. There are now a number of curriculum mapping software programs that take mapping beyond merely recording and accessing curriculum data, to allowing users to perform sophisticated tasks that greatly expand and enhance the mapping process. Users can perform searches for keywords, specific topics, units of study, skills, standards, and assessment strategies. Aligning content and/or skills to preloaded state academic standards is a common feature that saves time. Teachers can access national databases for assessment strategies and lesson ideas. Reports can be generated that assist teachers and administrators to determine curriculum patterns and trends. Most recently, there are steps to link curriculum mapping software programs with other data systems software programs—allowing all users to efficiently analyze and compare curriculum mapping and outcome data. These types of analysis help teachers and administrators make data-driven decisions to improve student learning and achievement.

For many educators, choosing a software program is a complex task. Figure 5.1 provides a list of criteria to consider when choosing curriculum mapping software. This criteria was generated from various curriculum leaders, technology experts, and teachers. These educators represented large and small schools; some were using a particular program, while others were in the process of choosing curriculum mapping software.

CURRICULUM MAPPING SOFTWARE PROGRAMS

As you become familiar with the criteria, you will want to explore the various curriculum mapping software programs available. The following section offers

Figure 5.1   Criteria to Consider When Choosing Curriculum Mapping Software

TRAINING CONSIDERATIONS
What type of training opportunities will the software company provide?
Who will provide the training?
Are the trainers well trained in the curriculum mapping process as well as the software?
How will the training take place—on-site, by phone, other means?
How much front-end preparation time will be required by our district?
DATA INPUT—EASE OF USE
What is the process for entering the curriculum mapping data?
What is the process for modifying and entering existing curriculum data?
How customizable is the program? Will it be possible to add another section or change the file names?
Once the data are entered, are there multiple views available (e.g., landscape, vertical, only content, only skills, only assessments)?
How easily can users save their maps on disk?
What is the standards-alignment process offered in the software?
Are the particular state academic standards preentered into the software?
Can the standards be updated?
How are the administrative changes made?

DATA OUTPUT
Does the program have the capability of generating reports?
If yes, what types of reports?
How easily are the maps printed?
Can the maps be printed in various formats?
SUPPORT
What types of ongoing support will be available?
Is there an added cost for support?
Is 24-hour support available?
What types of help features are available (e.g., online, quick sheets, manual)?
What are the layers of access and security for teachers, administrators, students, parents, and community?
COST
What is the fee structure (e.g., initial cost, one-time fee with yearly updates, subscription fee)?
Is there an added cost for updating standards?
STABILITY OF COMPANY AND DATA OWNERSHIP
What other districts are using this software?
How long has the company been in business?
What is the company commitment to updating and improving the software?
Where is the software server actually located?
If the company hosts the software, who officially owns our curriculum maps?
If the company went out of business, how easy will it be for us to get our curriculum information?
EXISTING SYSTEM COMPATIBILITY
Is the software compatible with our local area network?
Is the software compatible with our existing hardware (dual platform)?
What amount of bandwidth is needed to run the program effectively and efficiently?
Will the local network be able to handle the demand?

a description of the most commonly used curriculum mapping software programs. The last program, Eclipse Curriculum Manager, is currently available only in Wisconsin. While the features of this program will be of particular interest to Wisconsin districts, the overall program components may provide useful comparison information beyond Wisconsin residents.

Curriculum Mapper

Created and designed by practicing K–12 educators, Curriculum Mapper is the oldest Web-based mapping system available. Curriculum Mapper works through an Internet browser and allows teachers to create, edit, search, and analyze curricular data from any computer with an Internet connection.

Key Features:

- Curriculum Mapper works on both Macs and PCs, and may be used with any of the three major browsers: Internet Explorer, Netscape, or Safari.
- It has a large searchable database of curriculum maps from over 40 states and Canada.
- Teachers can attach documents and files to their maps and decide who is allowed to view those attachments.
- It offers reporting tools that allow schools to track where and when—and how deeply—standards are addressed.
- It allows teachers to indicate and track where identified standards were introduced, developed, or reinforced, to give a more complete picture of the curriculum.
- All maps can be exported at any time to a Microsoft Word document or database-ready file.
- All reports are three-dimensional and allow users to zoom in on all relevant maps to get more information.

Administrators and teachers benefit from the comprehensive analysis tools and reports. For more information, contact Curriculum Mapper at www.curriculummapper.com.

Technology Pathways

TechPaths is a curriculum mapping system designed for systems thinking and continuous improvement. The TechPaths system isolates the key elements that lead to successfully creating a standards-based curriculum.

Key Features

Data Entry and Standards Alignment

- It is a user-friendly process for entering key map elements.
- Standards and benchmarks are customized in the software and easily aligned to the curriculum data entered by pointing and clicking on the appropriate standard.

Reports Feature

- Consolidated reports can be generated that provide a summary of all data that have been entered with available frequency counts.
- Administrative reports can be created that serve as a guide for professional development, supervision, and coaching. The same reports that are available to teachers are available to administrators by department, building, or district.

Search Feature

- Teachers can search to see other teachers' maps.
- Teachers can use the tracker report to see how frequently they addressed specific skills or content that were on the state standardized tests.
- Users are able to search at the following levels: course, department, building, district, international.

TechPaths Libraries

- All lessons and assessments are archived and form a library of resources for teachers in the district. An enhancement is available in which teachers can have access to sets of performance assessment tasks that can be used for district benchmarks or for classroom assessments.

Performance Tracker Partnership

TechPaths partners with a data mining system that provides reports based on standardized and standards-based tests. The reports drill down to the classroom and the individual student. When districts commit to this partnership, there is a link between TechPaths and Performance Tracker so that teachers can seamlessly move between the two applications. For more information, contact Technology Pathways International at www.Techpaths.com.

Rubicon Atlas Curriculum Management Software

Rubicon works with public and private schools worldwide to plan and implement curriculum mapping initiatives using Atlas, the firm's Web-based curriculum management software. Atlas is customized to meet each school or district's unique needs.

Atlas is a comprehensive management tool with the ability to analyze curriculum, align to standards, link to student assessment data, and share curriculum and best practices with other schools around the world.

Key Features

- It is customized to accommodate each school's mapping approach and goals.
- It incorporates individual, collaborative, or master maps.
- It allows "planner views" for schools using special templates.
- It links Web sites, lesson plans, and other resources to maps.

- It includes notes that are fully integrated with school e-mail.
- It incorporates the ability to map and analyze unique areas of endeavor such as school values, strategic plans, or differentiated instruction.
- It includes a customized parents' site.

For information, contact Rubicon Atlas at www.rubiconatlas.com.

Eclipse Curriculum Manager

The Eclipse Curriculum Manager is a Web-based application designed to map and manage a district's curriculum.

Key Features

- The Eclipse Curriculum Manager is offered on a perpetual license basis, meaning a district pays once and the software license allows the district to use the software indefinitely.
- The company offers on-site training for teachers and administrators.
- Teachers can analyze where and how often the Wisconsin State Standards and local Benchmarks are taught within the curriculum.
- It works on both PCs and Macs, and may be used with the Mozilla, Firefox, Safari, Netscape, and Internet Explorer Web browsers.
- It easily allows for customization to meet the individual district's curriculum needs.
- It has the ability to attach supporting documents and files to their course curriculum.
- It includes a lesson plan format.
- Maps are easily available for all teachers to view.
- The report component generates various types of reports that compares curriculum within and across multiple grades and courses.
- Users have the option to share desired map elements with the local community.
- It is based on open source technologies to reduce costs to districts engaged in the mapping process.
- It is based in Wisconsin and works exclusively with Wisconsin schools.

For more information, contact Eclipse Academic Systems LLC at info@ eclipseacademic.com.

Although incorporating curriculum mapping software is highly recommended, there are challenges to be considered. It will take time and resources for teachers to learn the software program. Additional time will need to be built into the curriculum mapping implementation plan. Some teachers will be hesitant to learn the software and will need additional support. While all teachers will receive training, usually by representatives of the software company, it is recommended that key teachers receive additional in-depth training. Those teachers can become the "go-to" resources and can provide assistance within specific buildings.

Curriculum mapping technologies have facilitated widespread communication capabilities across buildings, districts, the country, and the world. Teachers and administrators now have the capacity to analyze maps to greater degrees of sophistication and to link the curriculum data with other schoolwide data sources for informed decision making. This potential has far-reaching positive implications for improved teacher performance and student achievement. While all schools involved with curriculum mapping may not have the resources to purchase a curriculum mapping software program, it is highly recommended that it be a serious consideration as curriculum mapping is continued.

Conclusion

Curriculum mapping is a multilayered, complex journey that requires a strong foundation, shared leadership, external assistance, and an understanding that curriculum is never finished. While the process of curriculum mapping begins with the goal of creating authentic curriculum maps, the value goes far beyond creating good curriculum. I have learned that as educators progress through the steps of curriculum mapping, they build professional relationships, analyze their own and others' beliefs about teaching, and create more meaningful learning environments for students. It is an ongoing process that changes and evolves as our learning and circumstances change and evolve.

Writing this book was much like the process of curriculum mapping. It created opportunities for me to collaborate with other professionals and reflect on my own beliefs about teaching, learning, and curriculum building while focusing on what is most beneficial and practical for teachers and students. I've discovered that just as the maps are never finished, this book is difficult to wrap up in a tidy conclusion. This final section doesn't really mark the end but, rather, indicates a temporary, reflective stopping point. There are many more stories to be told, more experiences to share, perspectives to consider, and new mapping avenues to discover.

Many schools benefit from embarking on the curriculum mapping journey. There will emerge new areas of curriculum mapping to be developed and explored. As more teachers are mapping and the technological capabilities advance and improve, the possibilities for sharing maps and creating collaborative, professional relationships beyond district boundaries to state, national, and international levels are astounding. Data management software companies are developing new products that will coordinate with mapping data that hold great promise for more efficient analysis and consequently more meaningful action. These are exciting areas that hold great opportunity and promise for continued learning and growth.

Appendix

The following pages include a variety of map samples. Some of the samples illustrate maps in progress where the content, skills, and assessments are included but the essential questions and/or academic standards have not yet been completed. Those sections are to be finished as the mapping cycle continues. Other samples include activities and/or resources, which were referred to in Chapter 3. It is also noted that some maps follow a slightly different format where the component titles are listed down the left margin instead of across the top. The format makes little difference as long as all components are included.

These samples provide illustrations of various content areas and grade-level maps, the connection between content, skills, and assessments, the use of action verbs when describing skills, and a combination of assessments. Anecdotal commentary is included on the samples pointing out map variations.

Sample A.1   Kindergarten Vocal Music Curriculum Map

This sample includes more than one month that is especially common in related arts courses and includes the resources component—Musical selections.

	August	September	October	November	December
Essential Questions	• How can I show a steady beat? • What are the four ways I can use my voice? • How do I prepare my body for singing?	• How can I show steady beat? • What are the four ways I can use my voice? • Why are loud/soft important in a song?	• How can I show steady beat? • What are the four ways I can use my voice? • Why are loud/soft important in a song?	• How can I show steady beat? • Why are loud/soft important in a song? • In what directions can notes in a melody move?	• How can I show steady beat? • Why are loud/soft important in a song? • How can notes be grouped or organized?
Content	• Vocal tone color • Steady beat • Vocal/Physical preparations (warm-up)	• Dynamics	• Steady beat	• Steady beat • Pitch	• Steady beat • Duration/notation (long/short)
Skills	• Identifies and uses all four voices (speaking, calling, whispering, singing) • Pats the steady beat; plays the steady beat on a drum	• Plays unpitched instrument loudly or softly • Sings a song using loud/soft voice • Moves to show loud/soft	• Plays steady beat on non-pitched instrument	• Sings a song to determine melodic direction • Moves hands/arms to show upward and downward	• Speaks slowly/quickly • Makes long/short movements • Identifies/follows picture representation of long/short
Assessments	• Echo-speak with inflection • Echo-sing short phrases • Listen to a selection and move body parts to the beat	• Listen to a selection and identify loud/soft sounds using body movement • Perform selections using the four types of voices and demonstrating use of loud/soft	• Listen to selection and play nonpitched instrument to steady beat	• Listen and move to show melody moving upward/downward • Follow pictorial notation and sing upward/downward melody shape	• Sing with long, sustained sounds and then short sounds • Listen to selection, following pictorial notation and show long/short through body movement
Musical Selections	• "Hello Everybody" • "See You Later" • "Round in a Circle" • "March From Summer Day Suite"	• "Play the Drum" • "Johnny Works With One Hammer"	• "Wee Willie Winkie" • "Make Me Shake Me" • "Down by the Bay"	• "Bear Hunt" • "Brush Your Teeth" • "The Roller Coaster" • "Wee Willie Winkie"	• Holiday/winter selections

SOURCE: Reprinted with permission of the author, Kim Sidwell-Frame, Vocal Music Teacher, Ankeny Community Schools. Reproduction authorized only for the educational institution that has purchased this book.

80

Sample A.2 Second Grade Math Curriculum Map

This curriculum map is a first draft and lists the topic and content as two separate components. The essential questions and state standards will be included as the mapping cycle continues.

11 Essential questions	Topic	Content	Skills	Assessments	State Standards
	(September) Mathematical Process	• Problem solving	• Write number sentences for given addition or subtraction story problems	• (Test—written) Assessment Lessons 15, 20, and 30 Tests—from text. • (Worksheet) Class practice page • (Observation) Journal practice problems • (In-class discussion) Oral answers • Completed bar graph	
	(September) Number Operations and Relationships	• Number order • Number computing • Ordinal numbers • Even and odd numbers • Property	• Identify and write number order to 100 • Compute addition fact doubles • Select ordinal positions of given objects to 12 • Compare number sizes to 50 • Order numbers by size • Add basic number facts involving 0, 1, and 2 • Apply associative property of addition • Identify even and odd numbers	• (Test—written) Assessment Lessons 10, 15, and 20 Tests—from text. • (Worksheet) Daily homework page • (Observation) Journal practice problems • (Discussion) Classroom flash cards • (In-class discussion) Daily math meeting	
	(September) Geometry	• Shapes • Area	• Identify shape attributes • Use pattern blocks to determine area	• (In-class discussion) Oral comparison • (Worksheet) Class practice • (Test—written) Assessment Lesson 25 Test—from text	
	(September) Measurement	• Time • Calendar	• Read and show time to the hour • Read calendar date correctly (daily)	• (In-class discussion) Oral answers and class practice • (Test—written) Assessment Lesson 25 Test—from text	
	(September) Statistics and Probability	• Graphing	• Complete a bar graph for given information	• (In-class discussion) Daily math meeting • (Worksheet) Class practice page	
	(September) Algebraic Relationships	• Patterns	• Create a pattern block design • Create and read a repeating pattern • Complete a repeating pattern (daily)	• (Worksheet) Class practice page • (In-class discussion) Oral answers • (Test—written) Assessment Lesson 20—from text • (In-class discussion) Daily math meeting	

SOURCE: Reprinted with permission of the author, Lori Stietz. Reproduction authorized only for the educational institution that has purchased this book.

Sample A.3 Second Grade Reading Curriculum Map

This map includes resources and activities. The component titles are along the left margin instead of across the top as in Sample A.2. Standards have not yet been aligned and added.

Month		September	
Essential Questions	• What is the word? • How can I figure out words I don't know?	• What is fluent reading? • Why is it important to read fluently? • How can reading fluently help me understand what I'm reading?	• Why is it important to understand a story? • What helps me to understand a story I've read?	• What helps me to understand a story I've read?
Content	• Decoding	• Fluency	• Comprehension • Vocabulary (word meaning)	• Literacy (story) elements

Skills	• Recognizes sight words through Level 9 automatically
	• Uses phonics rules
	  – Variable consonant sounds
	  – Blends and digraphs
	  – Long and short vowels and all rules
	  – Controlled vowels
	  – Pre/suffix/base words
	  – Inflectional endings
	  – Contractions
	  – Compound words
	• Applies decoding strategies: chunking, rhymes, pictures, context, rereads, builds on prior knowledge, read on, self-corrects
		• Recognizes and applies punctuation in oral reading
		• Shows expression in their reading
		• Uses a combination of all cueing systems
		• Reads with meaningful phrases
		• Uses sight words for fluent reading
			• Predicts before and during reading
			• Connects cause and effect
			• Compares and contrasts text
			• Identifies sequence of a story
			• Draws conclusions from text and picture
			• Recalls important details
			• Identifies main idea
			• Understands purpose for reading
			• Asks questions before, during, and after reading
			• Makes a connection to what is read
			  – text to text
			  – text to self
			  – text to world
				• Identifies main characters
				• Identifies setting
				• Identifies supporting characters
				• Identifies problem/solution

82

Month			September	
Assessments	• Benchmark assessment • Anecdotal records • Running records • Teacher observation	• 1-minute reading • Anecdotal records • Teacher observation • Guided reading oral reading • Sight word list • Benchmark assessments	• Story mapping • Oral retelling • Stand-up Triorama • Venn diagram • Vocabulary sentence activities • Benchmark assessments	• Story map • Book reports • Retell/oral discussion • Benchmark assessments
Resource	• *Making Words* book by Cunningham • *Words Matter* book by Fountas and Pinnell • Title I games • Guided reading books • Anthology books • Reading software, e.g., Rigby	• Reading Rainbow • Oskaloosa Storybook Players • Parent volunteers • Guest readers • CD-ROMs/cassette tapes • Anthologies • Guided reading books	• Guided reading books • *Making Words* by Cunningham • Big books • PM stories software (Rigby) • ELL instructors • *Mosaic of Thought* by Ellin Keene • *Strategies That Work* by Stephanie Harvey	• Big books • Author studies • Shared reading stories and anthologies • Thematic books • Guided reading books

SOURCE: Reprinted with permission of the author, Jan Keese & 2nd Grade Teachers, Ankeny Community Schools. Reproduction authorized only for the educational institution that has purchased this book.

Sample A.4 Third Grade Social Studies Curriculum Map

This completed map includes all components of a curriculum map.

Month	Essential Questions	Content	Skills	Assessments	Standards
September	Why are maps important? Why do we need different types of maps? What information is needed on a map?	Map Skills	Describe and identify map symbols and map key Locate east, west, north, and south on a map Identify a compass rose on a map Find distance in miles on a map using a map scale Compare and contrast political maps, physical maps, climate maps, and product maps Use a map grid to find locations on a map Create maps displaying a map key, map symbols, map scale, map grid, and compass rose	Worksheet/homework In-class activity worksheet/homework Identify displayed maps, complete activity sheet Worksheet/homework Mapmaking project with scoring rubric	A.4.1 Use reference points, latitude and longitude, direction, size, shape, and scale to locate positions on various representations of the earth's surface
October		Globe Skills	Locate the prime meridian and equator on a globe and flat map Locate the four hemispheres present in our world Identify and locate the seven continents, four oceans, and five major mountain systems Compare and contrast the size of the seven continents Create a map of the world illustrating the seven continents, the four oceans, and five major mountain systems Use latitude and longitude to find locations on a globe or flat map	Map activity sheet (in class) homework Map activity sheet (in class) Performance assessment: completed map Quiz	A.4.2 Locate on a map or globe physical features such as oceans, continents, mountain ranges

Sample A.5 Seventh Grade Science Curriculum Map

Like Sample A.2, this map illustrates the topic and content listed as two categories. The essential questions and standards will need to be completed as the mapping cycle continues.

Month	Essential Questions	Topic	Content	Skills	Assessments
September		• Science skills • Classification of Living Things	• Lab safety • Science vocabulary • Classification system • Binomial nomenclature • Insect structure • Insect classification	• Read and sign Flinn Scientific's Student Safety Contract • Locate and identify safety equipment • Apply safety rules in lab situations • Decipher the meaning of large science terms • Develop vocabulary for classification • List the groups in our modern classification system in sequence • Compare common and scientific names • Use dichotomous keys to identify objects/organisms • Collect and pin a variety of insects • Use field guides to identify insects • Classify insects in collections to order level • Identify the body structures of an insect	• (Letter) Signed lab safety contract • (Quiz) Lab safety quiz (Worksheet) • Worksheet: "Little Big Words" • (In-class discussion) Class discussion of science vocabulary • (Quiz) Quizzes on insect classification (Worksheet) • Worksheet: creature identification • (Teacher observation) Lab practice pinning and labeling insects • (Quiz) Insect structure quiz • (Graphic organizer) Comparison of metamorphosis • (Test—written) classification test

(Continued)

Sample A.5 (Continued)

Month	Topic	Content	Skills	Assessments
September			• Recognize three insects that are listed as invasive species in Wisconsin	• (Rubric) Insect collection rubric
			• Make a graphic organizer using "inspiration" to compare complete and incomplete metamorphosis • Explain the impact insects have on humans	

Sample A.6   Eighth Grade English Curriculum Map—Newspaper Unit

This completed map includes all components of a curriculum map.

Month	Essential Questions	Content	Skills	Assessments	Standards

September	Why do people read the newspaper?
	
	How do readers influence what gets printed in newspapers?
	
	How do newspapers influence society?
	
	Is the newspaper a good source for news?
		Newspaper unit
		
		Newspaper sections
		
		Headlines
		
		News stories
		
		Feature Stories
		
		Editorial section
		
		Advertising
			Analyze and chart newspaper reading habits of our class
			  – how many students read the newspaper
			  – the specific sections read by students
			
			Identify the sections of a newspaper
			
			Identify different forms of headlines
			
			Compare and contrast difference between news stories and feature stories
			  – identify key features of each type of story
			  – identify writer bias
			
			Describe the parts of the editorial page
			Analyze an editorial piece
			  – letter to the editor
			  – editorial piece
			  – editorial cartoon
			
			Interpret and explain the structure and content of newspaper advertising
				Completed chart with written analysis
				  – scored using district writing rubric
				
				In-class parts of newspaper activity: students complete project worksheet
				
				News story and feature story: compare and contrast worksheet
				Class discussion: anecdotal record
				
				Written analysis of a chosen editorial piece (student choice)
				  – district writing rubric to assess
				
				Write a letter to the editor, an editorial, or create an editorial cartoon
				  – use district writing rubric to assess
				
				Write a classified advertisement
				  – use district writing rubric to assess
					E.8.1 Work with data in the context of real-world situations
					E.8.2 Organize and display data from statistical investigations
					A.8.3 Read and discuss literary and nonliterary texts to understand human experience
					A.8.4 Read to acquire information
					B.8.1 Create or produce writing to communicate with different audiences for a variety of purposes
					B.8.2 Plan revise, edit, and publish clear and effective writing
					B.8.3 Understand the function of various forms, structures, and punctuation marks of standard American English and use them appropriately in written communication
					B.8.3 Participate effectively in discussion

Sample A.7 Ninth Grade Physical Science Curriculum Map

The standards will need to be added as the mapping cycle continues

	August/September	October	November	December
Essential Questions	• What processes keep scientific knowledge constantly changing? • Why is accuracy so important in science? • What makes an experiment valid and useful? • What are properties of matter?	• How can properties and interactions of matter help us identify substances? • What principles govern the interaction of matter? • What systems of organization are used to classify matter? • How can chemical reactions affect my life?	• How does the chemical structure of matter determine the properties of matter? • How do we determine the models of atoms and molecules?	• What holds matter together? • What determines the organization of the periodic table? • What are the characteristics of a solution? • What factors affect the characteristics of a solution?

Content	• Nature of science
	  – Science skills and methods
	  – Lab techniques and safety
	  – Accurate measurement
	• Nature of matter
	  – Properties of matter
		• Nature of matter
		  – Classification of matter
		• Interactions of matter
		  – Chemical reactions
		  – Chemical formulas
			• Nature of matter
			  – Structure of matter
			  – Atoms, molecules, elements, and compounds
				• Interactions of matter:
				  – Periodic trends
				  – Bonding
				  – Solution

Skills	• Identifies and uses science skills and methods • Describes and designs a controlled experiment • Uses proper and safe lab techniques • Compares volume, mass, and density • Measures mass, length, volume, and temperature • Differentiates between chemical and physical properties and changes • Compares and contrasts states of matter	• Classifies materials as elements, compounds, and mixtures • Distinguishes between heterogeneous and homogeneous matter • Separates mixtures using basic laboratory techniques • Describes evidence of a chemical reaction • Identifies reactants and products in a chemical reaction • Distinguishes between subscripts and coefficients	• Explains how the conceptual model of the atom has changed over time • Calculates the numbers of protons, neutrons, and electrons using the periodic table • Identifies pairs of atoms as isotopes	• Classifies elements as metals, metalloids, and nonmetals • Interprets the properties of an element based upon its position on the periodic table • Describes the role of electrons in chemical bonding

Sample A.7 (Continued)

	August/September	October	November	December
Skills	• Determines the density of solids, liquids, and gases • Describes the relationship in Boyle's and Charles's Laws	• Communicates what happens during a chemical change by writing a chemical equation • Identifies the four major types of chemical reactions (synthesis, decomposition, single replacement, and double replacement) • Explains what a chemical formula represents • Predicts a chemical formula for a compound given oxidation numbers	• Predicts electron configuration in neutral atoms	• Explains why atoms form chemical bonds • Infers the relationship between chemical bonds and chemical changes • Constructs a model of an atom using an electron dot diagram
Assessments	• Lab safety test • Glass cutting, shaping lab • Measuring volume and mass of solids and liquid lab • The mass of a gas lab • Product testing performance-based task • Design controlled experiment lab • Density lab	• Self-knowledge inventory prepost check for understanding • Concept map "What I know about chemicals!" (pretest) • Conducting a survey on chemical use and understanding • Adopt an element lab • Separating a mixture lab • Qualitative and quantitative water-quality testing (local water sources) (Optional)	• Model construction "Atomic Model" • Chemical reaction labs • Element brochure—performance-based task • Essay-style evaluation (student selects 4 questions from pool of 7–8)	• Chemical interaction labs • Synthesis, decomposition, single replacement, and double replacement labs • Experimental design lab • Double-blind lab • Saturated and supersaturated solutions labs • Qualitative analysis—performance-based task • Crime scene investigation—performance-based task

SOURCE: Reprinted with permission of the author, David Glenn, Science Teacher, Ankeny Community Schools. Reproduction authorized only for the educational institution that has purchased this book.

Sample A.8   Grades 9/10 Physical Education Curriculum Map

This essential questions component will need to be completed as the mapping cycle continues.

Month	Content	Skills	Assessments	Standards
November	Volleyball	Demonstrates volleyball skills: bumping, digging, setting, spiking, blocking, overhand serve, player position, and rotation Understands and applies volleyball rules and regulations Explains and applies various game strategies	Skills test: individual and group Written exam: objective Essay exam to explain strategies and various game scenarios. Correct grammar will be assessed as well as content.	The physical education standards will be added as the initial mapping cycle continues.
December	Basketball	Demonstrates basketball dribbling, passing, shooting Explains offensive and defensive position and play Explains and applies basketball rules and regulations Applies various basketball-playing strategies	Skills test: individual and group Essay exam Observed performance: assessed using rubric	

Sample A.9 Grades 10–12 World History Curriculum Map

Essential questions will need to be added as the mapping cycle continues.

Month	Content	Skills	Assessments	Standards
September	Five themes of geography – location – place – interaction – movement – region Culture/Diffusion Civilizations – governments – economics – religions – languages Study skills	Identify and explain the five themes Recognizing and applying vocabulary related to the five themes of geography Explain types of movement Explain global interdependence Categorize types of regions Defining the terms *culture* and *diffusion* Recognize major time periods and civilizations Apply study and note-taking styles and skills	Essay describing themes and giving one example of each. District writing rubric used to assess writing. Oral questioning Objective vocabulary test Map test Globe, maps, charts worksheets, and performance activity Course notebook: periodic checks and assessment	A.12.1 Describing physical attributes of places or regions A.12.4 Analyzing short- and long-term effects of population changes A.12.5 How population changes influence geographic and environmental change A.12.8 Identify major world ecosystems and cultural systems B.12.13 Analyze examples of ongoing changes within and across cultures
October	Middle East – regions – nations – civilizations Study skills	Define key vocabulary terms Categorize types of regions of the Middle East Valuing interaction: people, land, and contributions Recognizing major time periods in the Middle East Explaining global interdependence Identify and label nations, capitals, and land forms Extracting and synthesizing information from a variety of resources (library and Internet)	Vocabulary quiz Objective test (true/false, multiple choice and essay questions) Essay explaining interaction and global interdependence Map test Small group project with oral presentation – teacher and peer assessed	B.12 Historical eras or themes A.12.5 (See above) A.12.6 Analyzing geographic information A.12.8 (See above) E.12.1 Use computers to acquire and organize information

SOURCE: Reprinted with permission of the author, Greg Lage, Economics Teacher, Ankeny Community Schools. Reproduction authorized only for the educational institution that has purchased this book.

References

Barth, R. (2001). *Learning by heart.* San Francisco: Jossey-Bass.

Costa, A., & Kallick, B. (2004). *Assessment strategies for self-directed learning.* Thousand Oaks, CA: Corwin Press.

DuFour, R., & Eaker, R. (1998). *Professional learning communities at work: Best practices for enhancing student achievement.* Alexandria: VA: Association for Supervision and Curriculum Development.

English, F. (1980). Curriculum mapping. *Educational Leadership 37*(7), 558–559.

Forget, M. (2004). *MAX teaching with reading and writing.* Victoria, BC: Trafford Publishing.

Fox, D. (2001). Three kinds of data for decisions about reading. *Using data for educational decision-making: The newsletter of the Comprehensive Center 6*(1), 11–13.

Fullan, M. (2001). *Leading in the culture of change.* San Francisco: Jossey-Bass.

Garmston, R., & Wellman, B. (1999). *The adaptive school.* Norwood, MA: Christopher-Gordon Publishers.

Guskey, T. (2000). *Evaluating professional development.* Thousand Oaks, CA: Corwin Press.

Jacobs, H. H. (1997). *Mapping the big picture.* Alexandria, VA: Association for Supervision and Curriculum Development.

Jacobs, H. H. (2001). Procedures for curriculum mapping. In R. Burns (Ed.), *Curriculum renewal: Curriculum Mapping* (pp. 67 72). Alexandria, VA: Association for Supervision and Curriculum Development.

Jacobs, H. H. (2003). Connecting curriculum mapping and technology. *Curriculum Technology Quarterly, 12*(3), 1–4.

Jacobs, H. H. (2004). *Getting results with curriculum mapping.* Alexandria, VA: Association for Supervision and Curriculum Development.

Joyner, E. (2000). No more "drive-by" staff development. In P. Senge et al. (Eds.), *Schools that learn* (pp. 385–395). New York: Doubleday.

Karbon, J. (2004). Unpublished interview data.

Kostelanetz, R. (1986). In W. Lincoln and W. Suid (Eds.), *The teacher's quotation book* (p. 77). New York: Dale Seymour Publications.

Nevills, P. (2003). Cruising the cerebral superhighway. *Journal of Staff Development, 24*(1), 20–24.

Nicholas, E. (2004). *Developing consensus maps: Ways to adapt the mapping process developed by Heidi Hayes Jacobs.* Presentation at the Curriculum Mapping Midwest Regional Conference Improving Student Performance, Indianapolis, Indiana.

Rasmussen, C., Hopkins, S., & Fitzpatrick, M. (2004). Our work done well is like the perfect pitch. *Journal of Staff Development, 25*(1), 16–22.

Sargent, J. (2000). *Data retreat participant's guide.* Green Bay, WI: Cooperative Education Service Agency 7.

Senge, P., et al. (Eds.). (2000). *Schools that learn.* New York: Doubleday.

Solomon, P. (2003). *The curriculum bridge.* Thousand Oaks, CA: Corwin Press.

Steffy, B., & English, F. (1997). *Curriculum and assessment for world-class schools.* Lancaster, PA: Technomic Publications.

Udelhofen, S., & Larson, K. (2003). The mentoring year: A step-by-step guide to professional development. Thousand Oaks, CA: Corwin Press.

Wiggins, G., & McTighe, J. (1998). *Understanding by design.* Alexandria: VA: Association for Supervision and Curriculum Development.

Index

**CORWIN
PRESS**

The Corwin Press logo—a raven striding across an open book—represents the union of courage and learning. Corwin Press is committed to improving education for all learners by publishing books and other professional development resources for those serving the field of K–12 education. By providing practical, hands-on materials, Corwin Press continues to carry out the promise of its motto: **"Helping Educators Do Their Work Better."**